AF584767

NO WAY!

The Wildest Mind-Blowing Facts in the Universe

Dan Marshall

LOST
THE
PLOT

LOST
THE
PLOT

A Lost the Plot book, first published in 2021 by Pantera Press,
an imprint of Hardie Grant Publishing

Pantera Press
Gadigal Country
Level 7, 45 Jones Street
Ultimo NSW 2007

A Cataloguing-in-Publication entry for this book is available from the National Library of Australia.

ISBN 978-0-6486770-2-4 (Hardback)

Cover and internal design: Dan Marshall
Publisher: Martin Green
Editor: Anna Blackie
Proofreader: Tahlia Anderson

Printed and bound in China by Shenzhen Jinhao Color Printing Co., Ltd.

Pantera Press policy is to use papers that are natural, renewable and recyclable products made from wood grown in sustainable forests. The logging and manufacturing processes are expected to conform to the environmental regulations of the country of origin.

For Holly, Milly & Winnie.
xx

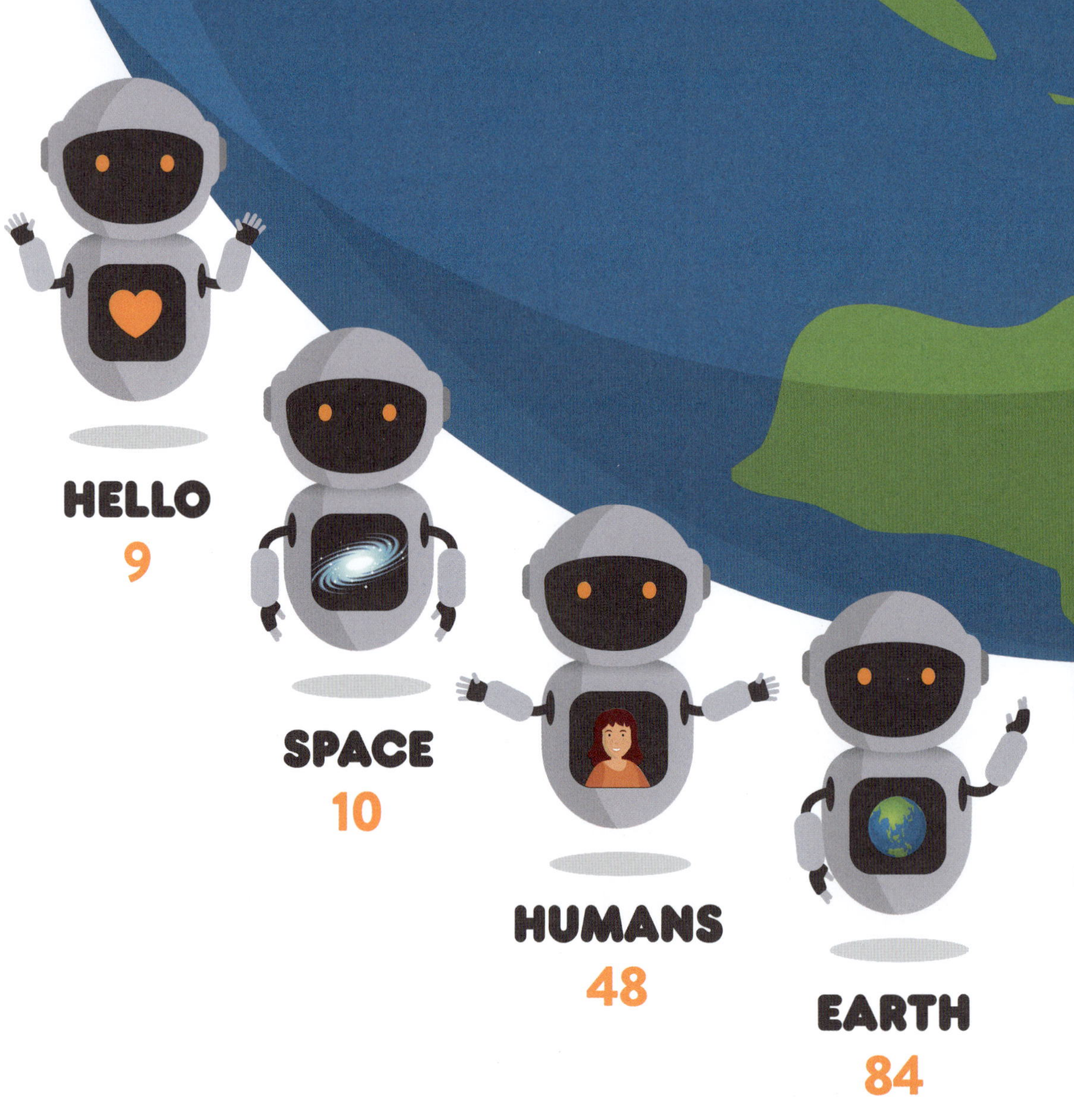

CONT

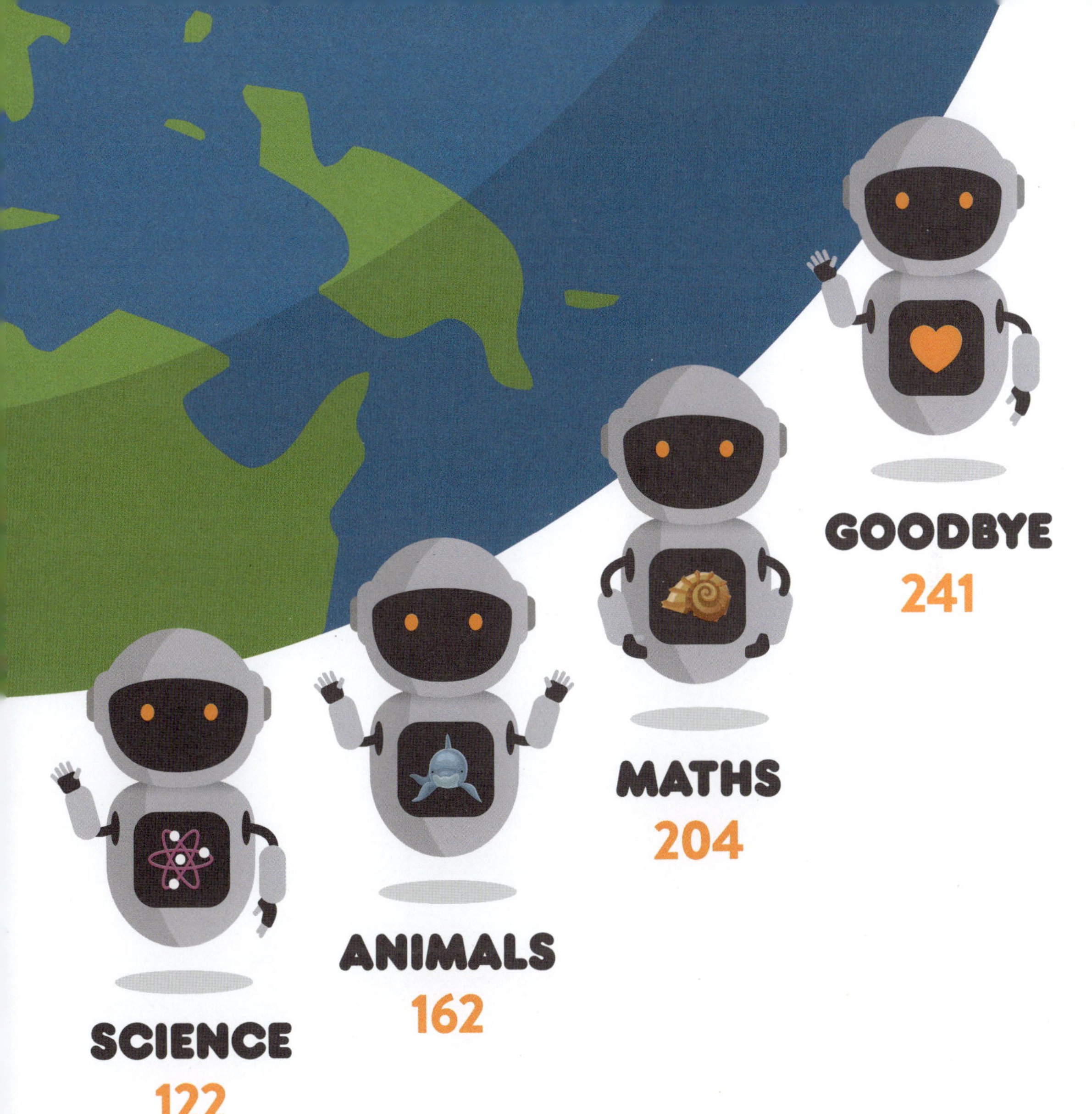

ENTS

Hello there,

My name is **KLAUS** (Knowledge Learning and Understanding System). I'm extremely excited that you have picked up this book and decided to go on an inspiring journey of discovery!

There are so many amazing facts about the weird and wonderful world around us, and I just can't wait to share them with you so that you can share them with other people too! Sharing is caring, after all.

As you fill your mind with all the fascinating new facts, there will also be challenges set to keep that brain working hard. You're going to love it, and I'll be right with you all the way to help you learn as we explore this wild universe together!

Brilliant, let's go!

THE MILKY WAY GALAXY IS ALMOST AS OLD AS THE UNIVERSE ITSELF

The spiral galaxy we call home, the Milky Way, is ancient – in fact, it's almost as old as the universe itself! The universe is about **13.7 billion years old**, while the Milky Way has been around for about **13.6 billion** (give or take another **800 million years**.) Not only is the Milky Way old, but it's ginormous too, measuring a whopping **100,000 light-years** in diameter – that's about **1,000,000,000,000,000,000 kilometres**!

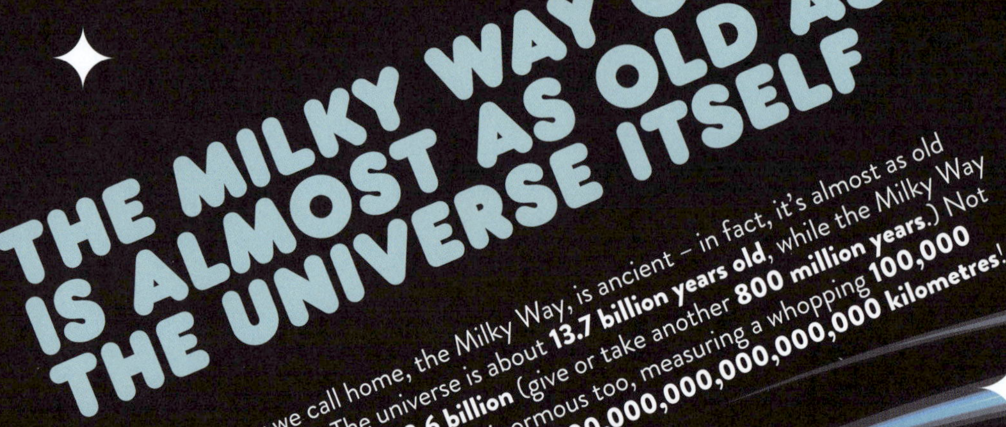

Take a moment to try to visualize just how humungous a **trillion** is. That's a **1** followed by **12 zeros**, **1,000,000,000,000**.

You can't read the label when you are inside the jar

Every picture you've ever seen of the Milky Way (including the one on this page) is just an artist's impression. Because we're inside the Milky Way, we can't actually take a picture of it from above – that would be like trying to take a picture of your own house from inside your bedroom.

An extremely ravenous beast

Don't be fooled by its pretty looks; the Milky Way is a savage! It's got a huge appetite and if another, smaller galaxy passes too close by, the Milky Way will rip it to shreds and ingest its stars and gas. Burp!

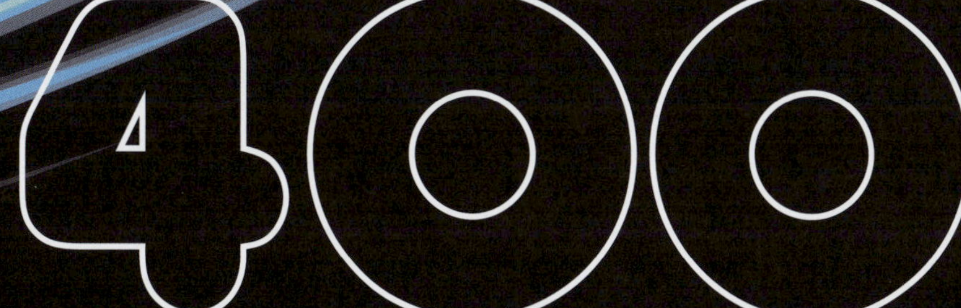

IT HAS OVER 400 BILLION STARS

When you look into the night sky, the most stars you can see from any one point on Earth is approximately **2500**. But did you know that the Milky Way actually has between **100–400 billion** stars? What we can see above us is only a fraction of that number. That may seem like a lot of stars, but there are other large galaxies which scientists believe may have as many as a trillion stars! The largest galaxy known, named **IC 1101**, has over **100 trillion** stars. No way!

THERE'S A BLACK HOLE AT THE CENTRE OF THE MILKY WAY WITH A MASS THAT'S FOUR MILLION TIMES THAT OF OUR SUN

A black hole is a place in space where gravity is so strong that all matter is pulled in. The strength of this gravitational pulls means that nothing can escape from within a black hole, not even light. The black hole at the centre of the Milky Way is a gravitational monster – it's so huge that we actually call it a **supermassive black hole**. Because no light can escape from a black hole, it's impossible to see this mega black hole, but what *can* be seen is matter being sucked away from the stars that stray too close to it.

Sooooooo many black holes

Scientists think the Milky Way galaxy is home to over **100 million black holes**, plus the supermassive monster one at the very centre. With somewhere between **200 billion** and **2 trillion** other galaxies in the universe, counting all the black holes would be an impossible task!

All shapes and sizes

There are four different sizes of black holes: **miniature**, **stellar**, **intermediate** and **supermassive**. The origins of supermassive and stellar black holes remain a mystery, but we know that intermediate black holes are created when a star dies, goes supernova and then collapses in on itself.

Miniature: These are theoretical, and scientists believe they may have formed when the universe was very, very young.

Stellar: These are the most common type of black holes and are formed when stars collapse at the end of their life.

Intermediate: These are theoretical cosmic middleweights, and are thought to have between a hundred and a million times the mass of the Sun.

Supermassive: These black holes at the centre of galaxies have between millions and billions more mass than the Sun.

Weird science

Things get pretty weird around black holes – not only does their gravitational pull make them invisible, but it's also so strong that it can *slow down time*! If you're unfortunate enough to be near a black hole, the laws of physics would go bonkers as space and time warped around you.

History was made in 2019, when a black hole was photographed for the first time! Well, sort of. Although we cannot see these cosmic beasts, we can see their edge. This is called the **event horizon**, and beyond that line our view of a black hole disappears entirely.

PEOPLE IN AUSTRALIA SEE THE MOON UPSIDE DOWN

No matter where they are in the world, everyone on planet Earth always sees the same side of the Moon. This is because the time it takes for the Moon to rotate on its axis is the same as the journey from one side of Earth to the other. While we may be seeing the same face of the Moon all across the world, if you live in the Southern Hemisphere you will see the Moon upside down compared to someone in the Northern Hemisphere.

SPACE CHALLENGE

Find out when the next full moon is. Look up and see if you can spot the **Sea of Tranquility** (also known as **Mare Tranquillitatis**) and draw it. Can you tell if you're in the Northern or Southern hemisphere?

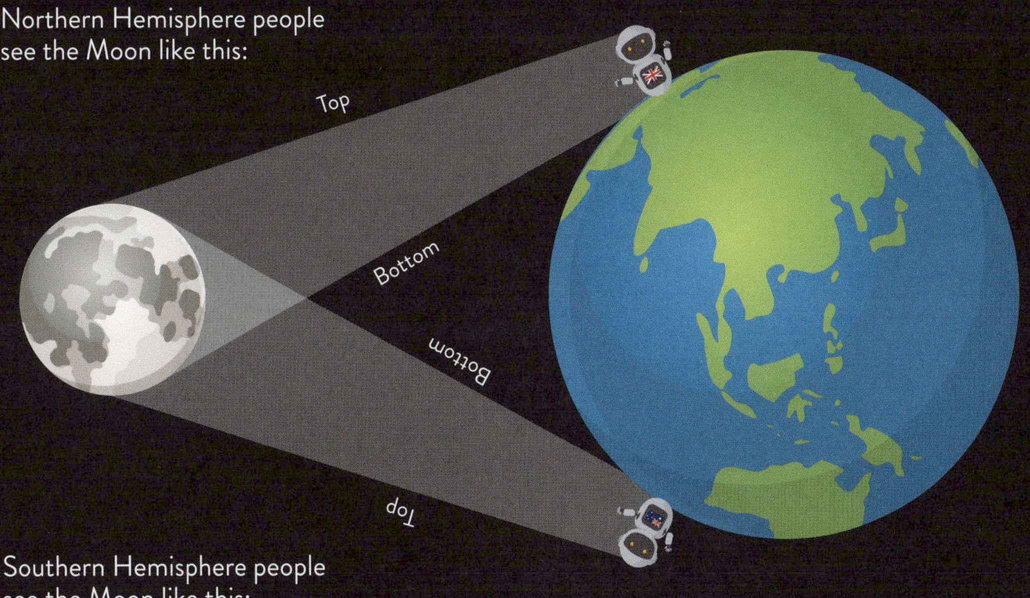

LIGHT TAKES 200,000 YEARS TO TRAVEL FROM THE CENTRE OF THE SUN TO ITS SURFACE, BUT ONLY 8 MINUTES TO REACH US ON EARTH

The sunlight we see on Earth is actually what the Sun looked like in the past – a whole **8 minutes** in the past, to be exact. While the 8-minute journey from the Sun to Earth might seem long, it's nothing compared to the **200,000 years** it took for that light to get from the Sun's core to its surface. All the atoms inside the Sun's core are squished tightly together, making it impossible for those atoms to find their way to the surface! The Sun is absolutely enormous, with a whopping radius of **700,000 kilometres**. Inside, the sunlight bounces around in all different directions before it finally breaks free and hurtles through space on its journey towards us on Earth.

Because the Sun is gradually brightening and expanding, it will one day absorb and destroy the Earth. But don't panic! In the last **4 billion years** the Sun has only expanded by around **20%**. And we've still got several billion years to go before things get too hot. Phew!

The cosmic speed limit

Did you know that space has a speed limit? Nothing we know of can travel faster than **the speed of light** in empty space, which is **300,000 kilometres per second**!

Earth times a million

The Sun is so huge that it takes up **99.86%** of the entire mass of the solar system – that's big enough to fit **1 million** Earths inside!

Not so cool bananas

The Sun's centre is **15 million degrees Celsius**, but even if it were made of bananas it would still be just as hot! The Sun is so hot because it contains a lot of mass squeezing down on its core. At these high temperatures all mass becomes plasma, meaning mass can be made of anything (even bananas!) and still be just as hot.

Light speed

If you could travel at the speed of light, you'd be able to go around the Earth **seven and a half times** in a single second. Wow!

NASA'S SPACE SHUTTLES WERE THE WORLD'S FIRST REUSABLE SPACECRAFT

NASA's 1981–2011 space shuttles were the heaviest and most expensive gliders ever built – they took off from Earth just like rockets, but returned home like gliders. The estimated total cost of the **30-year program** was an astronomical **US$209 billion**. As there were **5 shuttles** used during that time, the cost came to almost **US$42 billion per shuttle**.

The heaviest space shuttle orbiter, **Columbia**, weighed **80,700 kilograms**, which is roughly the same weight as **13 African elephants**. Throughout their **135 launches** the space shuttles carried large payloads, like satellites, into space. The shuttles' largest contribution was transporting astronauts and materials to help build the **International Space Station (ISS)**, which remains in orbit today.

28,000

The speed in kilometres per hour that the space shuttle travels as it orbits around Earth. At this pace, the crew are able to see a beautiful sunrise or stunning sunset every **45 minutes**.

355

The number of individual astronauts and cosmonauts who have flown on the space shuttle. This number is made up of **306 men** and **49 women** from **16 different countries**.

20,952

The total number of orbits around the Earth completed by all 5 space shuttles.

827 MILLION

The collective number of kilometres flown by all 5 space shuttles. That's more than the distance between Earth and Jupiter!

198,729

The total number of hours the space shuttles spent in space.

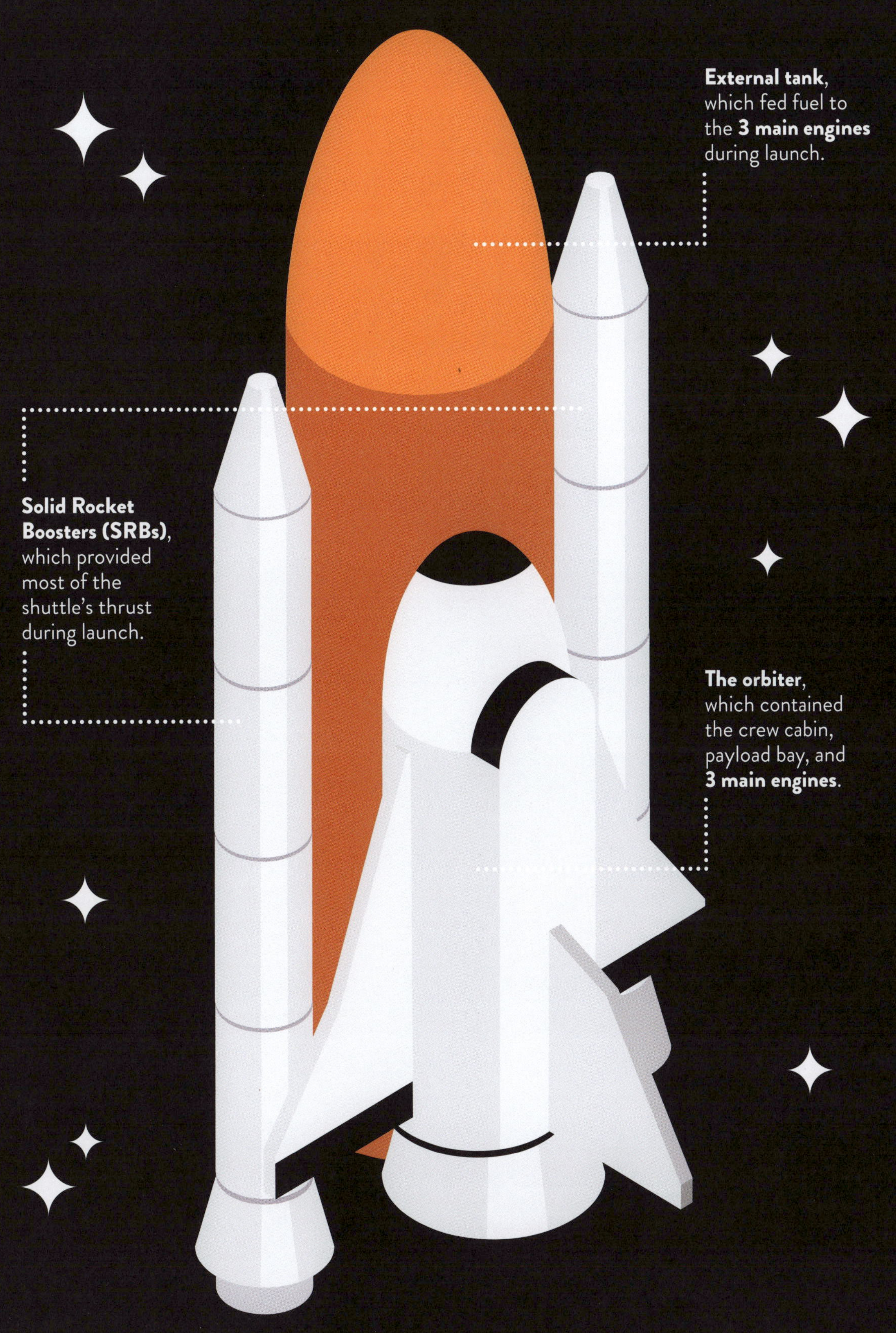
External tank, which fed fuel to the **3 main engines** during launch.
Solid Rocket Boosters (SRBs), which provided most of the shuttle's thrust during launch.
The orbiter, which contained the crew cabin, payload bay, and **3 main engines**.

ASTRONAUTS IN SPACE AGE SLOWER THAN PEOPLE ON EARTH

Astronauts on board the **International Space Station (ISS)** are orbiting Earth at an incredible **27,580 kilometres per hour**. Did you know that the faster you accelerate the more time slows down? Absolutely mind blowing, but we'll come back to that later in the book. After living onboard the ISS for **6 months**, any returning astronauts will have aged **0.007 seconds slower** than the rest of us here on Earth. This amazing effect is called **time dilation**.

These space adventurers may now *technically* be younger, but their bodies have actually experienced a fast-forwarding of the aging process as they whizzed around the Earth. Because of a lack of gravity, their muscles and bones lose strength and mass. One way these astronauts can help to reduce this degeneration is to use special exercise machines. It may look fun floating around in space, but these men and women have to hit the gym too!

Drink up

In order to survive onboard the ISS for a whole year, an astronaut must drink **730 litres of sweat and urine**. It may sound disgusting, but these astronauts' bodily fluids are recycled using a special filter that, over **8 days**, turns their waste into drinking water that is actually purer than the water that most of us drink at home. Delicious!

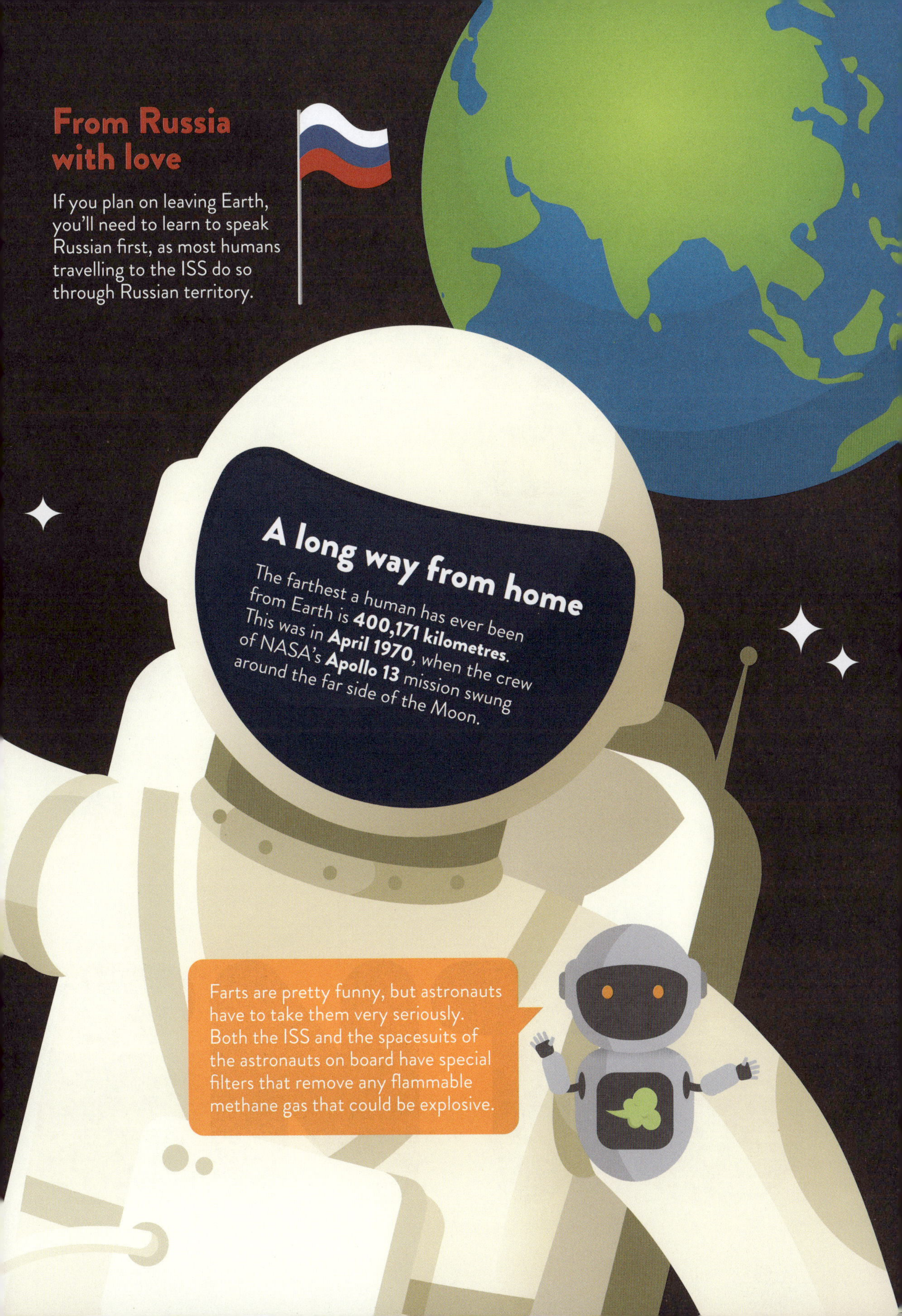

From Russia with love

If you plan on leaving Earth, you'll need to learn to speak Russian first, as most humans travelling to the ISS do so through Russian territory.

A long way from home

The farthest a human has ever been from Earth is **400,171 kilometres**. This was in **April 1970**, when the crew of NASA's **Apollo 13** mission swung around the far side of the Moon.

Farts are pretty funny, but astronauts have to take them very seriously. Both the ISS and the spacesuits of the astronauts on board have special filters that remove any flammable methane gas that could be explosive.

MOONMOONS ARE THE MOONS OF MOONS

We know that planets orbit stars and moons orbit planets, but did you also know that a moon can have an orbiting moon of its own? Scientists have yet to actually discover one, but they suspect that **moonmoons** must exist, as some moons in our solar system are bigger than actual planets, and most planets have moons!

A flying visit

We're able to swim in water because it is denser than air, so, in theory, if you had very thick air you could swim in it too – also known as flying! Saturn's largest moon, **Titan**, has an incredibly thick atmosphere combined with very low gravity. These conditions mean that if you made a set of wings and started flapping you would take off!

Many moons

Of all the planets in our solar system, **Saturn** is the one with the **most moons**. At last count, Saturn had **82 moons**, with Jupiter coming a very close second with a total of **79**.

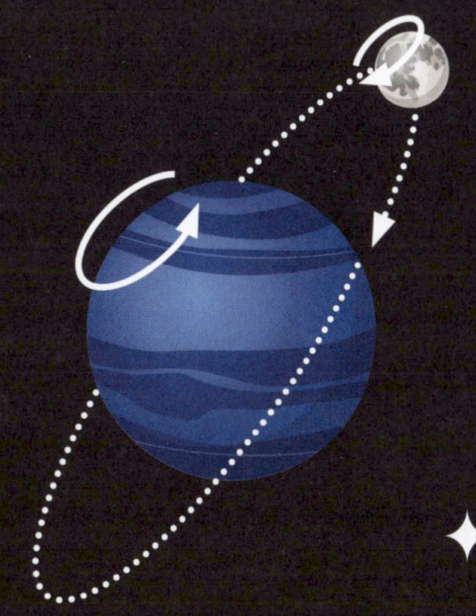

The total number of moons belonging to the various planets and dwarf planets in our solar system.

A change of direction

Triton is the largest of Neptune's moons. It's about the size of Earth's moon. Triton is the only moon of its size in the solar system with a **retrograde orbit** – that's when the moon orbits in the opposite direction to its planet's rotation.

Luna lava

Jupiter's moon, **Io**, has hundreds of volcanoes. Because of the incredibly strong gravitational forces on Io, the eruptions from these volcanoes can cause fountains of molten lava to explode up to **100 metres** into the sky!

552,894

The total number of asteroids in the solar system. These asteroids are mostly just chunks of rock that orbit the Sun; however, if they become captured by a planet's gravitational field and pulled into its orbit these rocks can become moons!

HOW HIGH CAN YOU JUMP ON OTHER PLANETS?

Put this book down for a moment and jump as high as you can. How high do you think you went?

No matter how high you jumped here on Earth, the varied masses and gravities of other planets mean that things are very different when you leap with the same force anywhere else in the solar system!

If you were to jump **0.5m metres** on Earth, the jump would only last a second.

EARTH

The gravity on the surface of the Moon is only **17%** that of Earth's. That means you could leap **3 metres** using the same force of a jump on Earth and you would remain in the air for about **4 seconds**.

MOON

Mars is larger than our Moon but smaller than Earth with about **33%** of its gravity. On Mars you could jump **1 metre** and stay in the air for **2 seconds**.

MARS

If you found yourself on **Comet 67P** it would actually be best if you *didn't* jump. If you did take the leap, you would just float off into the darkness of space. This is because your legs are strong enough to generate a jump that would break the rock's gravitational field, which would mean you'd achieve **escape velocity**. Away you go!

Saturn's moon Enceladus is only **14%** of the diameter of Earth's Moon. Jumping on this moon would be brilliant, as you would spring **43 metres** into the air. You would have plenty of time to enjoy it too, as it would take **60 seconds** to reach your peak before you floated back down to the surface.

Pluto may be a dwarf planet, but it's still pretty big! The surface gravity on Pluto is just **6%** that of Earth's, meaning a jump there would take you **8 metres high**, and last for **9 to 10 seconds**.

Escape velocity is the speed at which an object needs to be travelling in order to escape the pull of a planet's gravity. The escape velocity on Earth is **11 kilometres per second**!

PLUTO

ENCELADUS

COMET 67P

A long way round

Scientists believe it would take our mysterious ninth planet between **10,000** and **20,000 years** to orbit the Sun. They think this planet is about **20 times farther** from the Sun than Neptune, which completes an orbit roughly every **165 years**.

THERE MAY BE A MYSTERIOUS NINTH PLANET IN OUR SOLAR SYSTEM

At the far edge of our solar system, astronomers believe there may be an undiscovered planet, **Planet Nine**, lurking in the icy darkness. This hidden planet hasn't been located or photographed yet, but we have observed its **gravitational effect** on the odd orbits of distant space rocks.

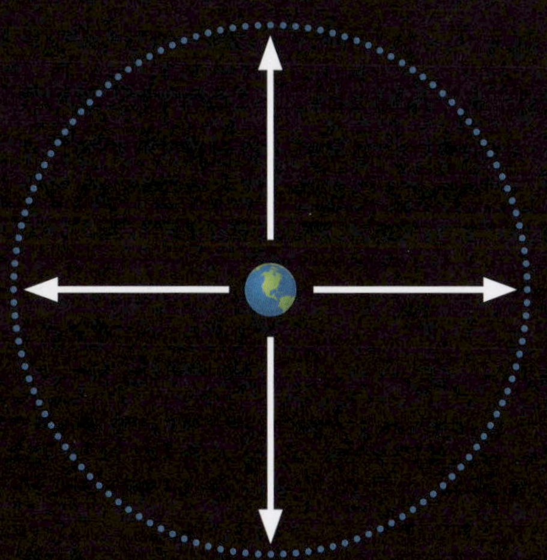

Your name up in lights

If, and when, the icy world of **Planet Nine** is found, the proper naming rights go to the person who discovers it. Planets are traditionally named after mythological Roman gods.

Earth times ten

The ninth planet could have a mass around **ten times** that of Earth. Possibly even more! Scientists have estimated this mass based on the strength of the potential planet's gravitational effect.

SPACE CHALLENGE

What would you name Planet Nine if you discovered it?

Cold enough for you?

Because the giant planet is so far from the Sun, it must get pretty cold there. It's suspected that the average temperature is a bone-chilling **-226°C**.

Hunting high and low

The further away from the Sun an object is, the harder it becomes to detect. However, we are using the world's most powerful telescopes to search for Planet Nine and are hopeful to one day discover it!

Some astronomers believe that rather than being a giant rogue planet, Planet Nine could actually be a tiny (but incredibly powerful) black hole – possibly as small as a baseball!

Roving robots

Much of the information we have about Mars is thanks to the robots who were sent there to explore and retrieve data. Because Mars is our closest neighbour (only **64 million kilometres** away!) it's the most robotically explored planet beyond Earth.

SPACE CHALLENGE

Would you be willing to leave Earth and travel for **7 months** through space to get to Mars? What would you take along on your cosmic journey?

Missing magnet

Earth is surrounded by a **protective magnetic field** that acts like a **force field**. Unlike Earth, Mars is missing this force field, which means that the Sun has stripped away most of the planet's atmosphere and left the frozen surface. Without this force field the Sun's heat easily escapes, leaving a burnt but chilly planet behind. Mars did once have a magnetic field of its own, but what happened to it remains a mystery.

MARS WAS ONCE COVERED IN WATER ...

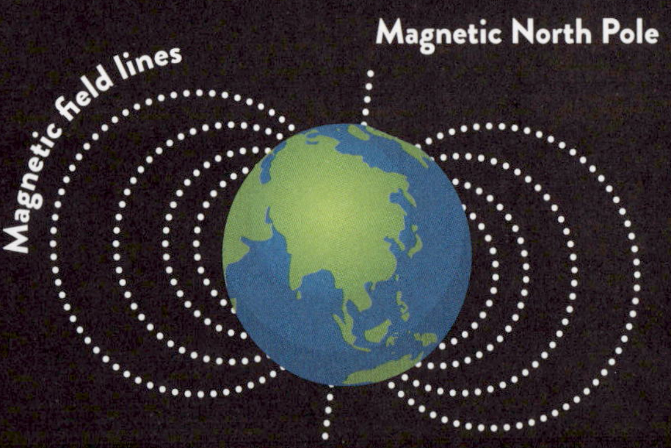

... AND HAD A THICK ATMOSPHERE, JUST LIKE EARTH!

Looking at these two neighbouring planets now – it's hard to believe that once upon a time Mars could have been mistaken for Earth's smaller twin. Instead of the rusty red surface that we see today, Mars was once covered in water, and maybe even life. No way!

This was billions of years ago, of course, and as well as oceans across the surface, Mars also had a thick atmosphere that kept it warm enough for the water to stay in liquid form. Today, this water is gone, although ice does remain in polar caps and beneath the red planet's surface.

Mission to Mars

Robots have set foot on Mars, and hopefully one day humans will join them! NASA is already planning Moon landing missions in preparation for a history-making journey to Mars. **Elon Musk**, the founder and CEO of **SpaceX**, has also declared his intentions to send humans to Mars, and is building a massive spacecraft called **Starship** to make the journey.

Mars is a planet with mountains, valleys and volcanoes. While Mars looks pretty similar to Earth on the surface, things are far more extreme on the red planet. **Olympus Mons**, the largest volcano on Mars, is three times the height of Mount Everest at an epic **22 kilometres**. It's also super wide, stretching **624 kilometres** across – Olympus Mons is so big that its slope curves with the surface of the planet!

Mars is also home to the **Valles Marineris** canyon system. These amazing valleys span over **4000 kilometres** and are **7 kilometres** deep – that's ***four* times** deeper and ***five* times** longer than the Grand Canyon!

ALL THE PLANETS IN OUR SOLAR SYSTEM CAN FIT BETWEEN EARTH AND THE MOON

Average distance between Earth and the Moon is **384,400 km**

Saturn **116,464 km**

Uranus **50,724 km**

Neptune **49,244 km**

Moon

Total diameters of Mercury + Venus + Mars + Jupiter + Saturn + Uranus + Neptune = **380,016 km**

If you added the diameters of every planet in our solar system (as per NASA's measurements, and with the exception of Earth) together they would equal **380,016 kilometres.**

That number may seem massive, but it's actually smaller than the distance between Earth and the Moon, meaning all the planets could fit in that space and have room to spare!

THERE IS LIGHT THAT WE ARE YET TO SEE

It's incredible to think that although we live in the universe, we're not able to see everything it contains because it's just so enormous! The universe is bigger than we can imagine, and everything exists inside it, including the Earth, planets, stars, space, galaxies, and even time. The part of the universe that we can see and detect from here on Earth is what we call the observable universe. Even though the portion of the universe we can see is relatively small, it still spans **93 billion light-years**!

We've been able to measure the distance of our observable universe based on the light that has travelled from its edge to Earth. From this we have also learnt that there is something beyond the observable universe (or the '**known universe**', as it's sometimes called). There will be light travelling there that has not yet reached Earth. In fact, there is way more of this light than the light we can actually see. What lies beyond there is a cosmic mystery that we one day hope to solve.

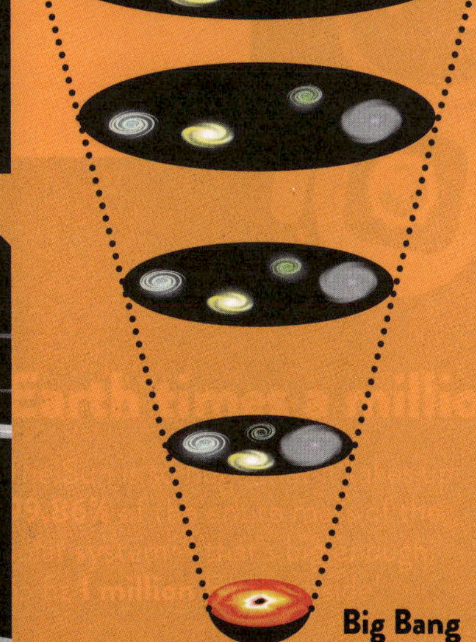

Did you know that the universe is constantly expanding? It's growing bigger and bigger all the time. And not only is the universe getting larger, but it is doing so at an increasingly fast rate. In fact, the edge of the universe is expanding faster than the speed of light!

Light-years

If you think driving to see your relatives takes a long time, try travelling across the universe! Because space is so massive, astronomers use the speed of light to measure how far away things are. A **light-year** is the distance that light can travel through space in **a year**, and we know this to be a whopping **9,460,000,000,000 kilometres**!

Nearest neighbours

The distance of our **Milky Way galaxy** from the next large galaxy, the **Andromeda galaxy**, is **21,000,000,000,000,000,000 kilometres**. That's a lot of zeros! To make it easier, we use light-years to measure this distance — **2.3 million light-years**, to be exact! Our nearest neighbouring star is **Proxima Centauri**, and this is much closer, with only a short **4.3 light-years** between us.

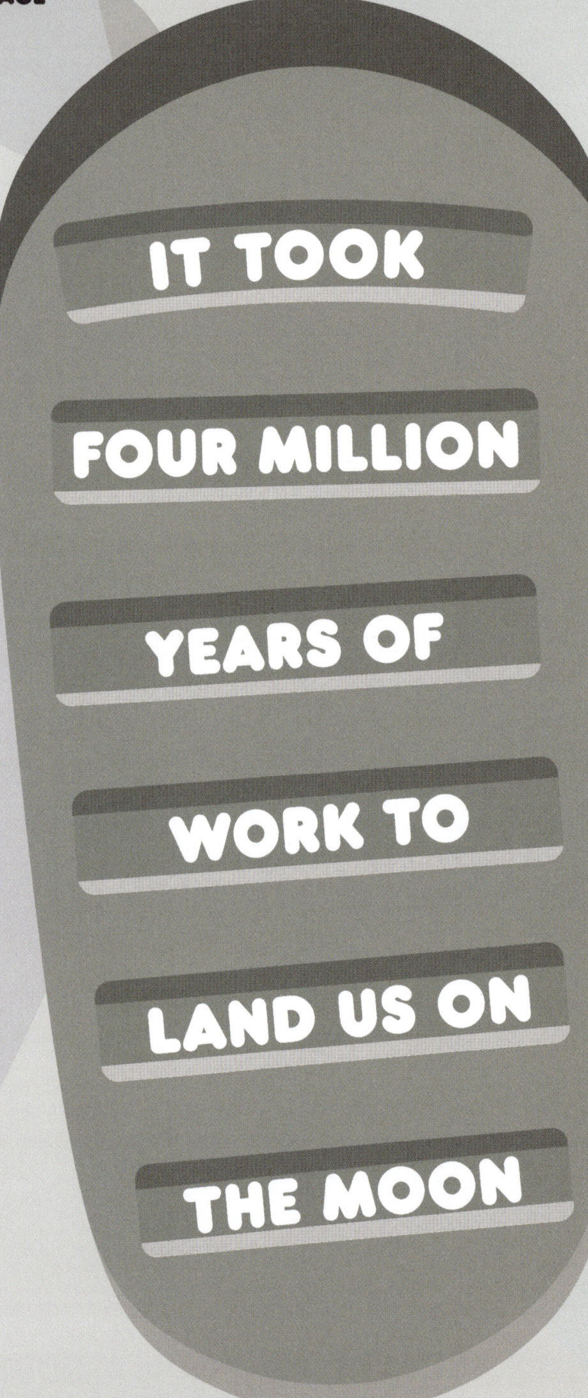

The **Apollo 11 moon landing** was made possible by **400,000 NASA workers**. These men and women worked tirelessly over a **10-year period** to make the Moon landing happen. It took a collective **4 million years** of work and **US$25 billion** to take humans to the Moon.

53 million households tuned in to watch the moon landing on their black and white televisions. That's an estimated **650 million viewers** worldwide!

The pen is mightier than the sword

After their triumphant landing, a broken switch onboard Apollo 11 meant the astronauts faced being stranded on the Moon. In a moment of inspiration, the astronauts inserted a felt-tip pen into the switch hole, activating the **ascent engine** and saving the day!

The **Apollo Lunar Module** was nicknamed **The Eagle**, and piloted by the Apollo 11 **mission commander**, **Neil Armstrong**. With the entire world watching, Armstrong missed the original landing site, but still managed to find an alternative area with less than a minute of descent fuel remaining. Close call!

Flag down

The first flag planted on the Moon by the Apollo 11 astronauts is probably no longer there. As the astronauts departed, the flag was knocked over by the lunar module's thrusters and has likely decomposed under the Moon's brutal conditions in the years since it was left behind.

Smell you later

Three astronauts stuck in a very tiny space were always going to get a little bit smelly, but did you know the hydrogen bubbles in their drinking water produced extra-gross farts? Things would have gotten pretty funky during that 8-day mission!

ASTEROID BELTS ARE LONELY PLACES TO BE

In movies, we see spaceships hurtling through asteroid belts, twisting, turning and generally doing their best to avoid a collision with the tightly packed chunks of space rock. But in reality, asteroid belts are a pretty lonely and boring place to be. The average distance between two asteroids on a belt is about **966,000 kilometres**. That's almost two and a half times the distance between the Earth and the Moon – think about how many planets could fit in that space! If you ever happened to find yourself on an asteroid, there would be only distant stars and the empty blackness of space to keep you company.

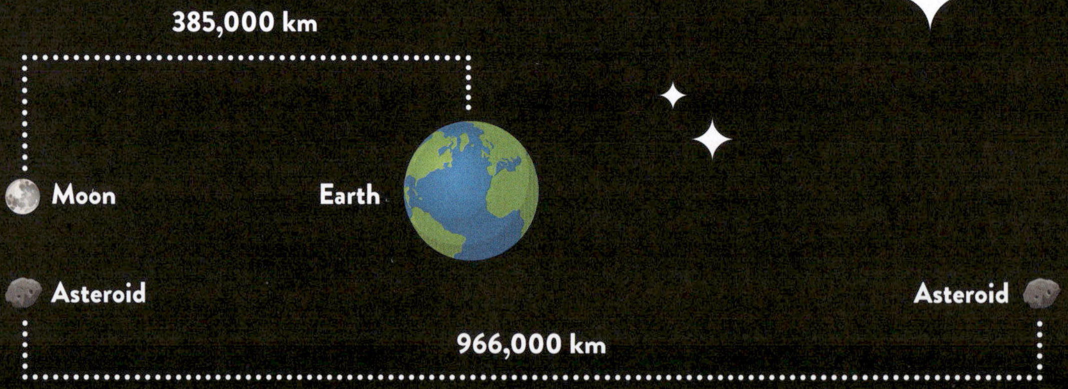

385,000 km

Moon

Earth

Asteroid

Asteroid

966,000 km

Rocking all over the word

The asteroid belt in our solar system can be found between the inner and outer planets, Mars and Jupiter. The belt contains **hundreds of thousands of asteroids**, but almost half of its entire mass is made up of just **four objects**. These are the three asteroids **Vesta**, **Pallas** and **Hygiea**, and the dwarf planet **Ceres**, which is a whopping **950 kilometres** in diameter.

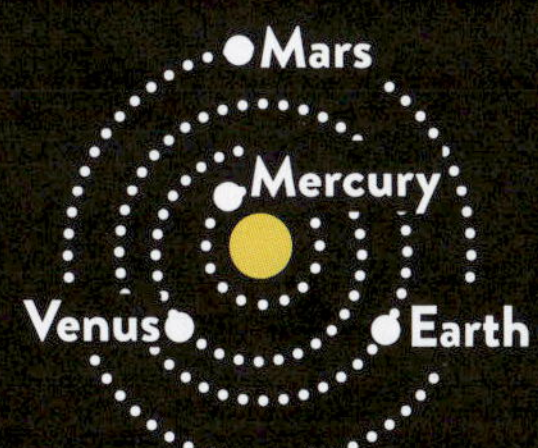

Dinosaur killer

Scientists agree that **66 million years ago** an asteroid between **10** and **80 kilometres in diameter** hit Earth, causing the extinction of the dinosaurs. The **Chicxulub Crater** is an impact crater **150 kilometres in diameter**, that was discovered under the **Yucatán Peninsula** in Mexico. This crater is believed to be the epicentre of the cataclysmic event.

SOMETHING IN DEEP SPACE IS SENDING SIGNALS TO EARTH

A mystery from a galaxy **500 million light-years** away has scientists scratching their heads. The galaxy is transmitting repeating radio signals that have reached Earth, but we don't yet know why, or who they're from!

Making waves

Radio waves are a kind of **electromagnetic radiation**, which means that they can move at the speed of light. However, they take a long time to travel through the mind-bending distance of space. The mysterious repeating signals have travelled **5 billion-trillion kilometres** over nearly **500 million years**. That's so long ago that when the signal began its journey, animals were only just beginning to emerge from Earth's oceans!

FRB 180916.J0158+65

This mouthful of numbers and letters is the name scientists have given the mysterious repeating signal.

Who or what do you think is sending the signals? Ideas range from **neutron stars**, **stars merging**, or even **black holes**. If you could communicate with the signal, what would you ask it?

Burst on the scene

The repeating signal is a type of **Fast Radio Burst** – that's where the FRB in the mystery signal's name comes from. These FRBs are mysterious deep-space signals, which are detected on Earth with radio telescopes. Usually, we detect these signals once and they are never heard from again, which is part of what makes FRB 180916.J0158+65 so unusual! Not only does it repeat, but it does so at regular intervals of **16.35 days**. For 4 days, the signal will emit a burst or two every hour. This is followed by 12 days of silence before the cycle repeats again.

URANUS IS LEAKING GAS INTO SPACE

A mysterious force is sucking Uranus's atmosphere out into space. When the **Voyager 2 space probe** flew past Uranus in 1986, it passed through a giant plasma bubble that had escaped from the planet and taken part of the atmosphere along with it. The giant plasma bubble was about **200,000 kilometres** long and twice as wide – that's ten times the circumference of Earth!

Poetic moons

Uranus's **27 moons** are all named after characters from the works of **William Shakespeare** and **Alexander Pope**, rather than figures in Greek and Roman mythology like the moons of other planets. The names include **Miranda**, **Ariel**, **Umbriel**, **Titania** and **Oberon**.

By George

When Uranus was first discovered in 1781 by William Herschel, he wanted to honour the king of the time, King George III, and named it **Georgium Sidus**. This name did not go down well with other scientists, and the planet was eventually renamed Uranus, after the Greek god of the sky. A shame, really, because as funny as Uranus may sound, 'Planet George' sounds even funnier!

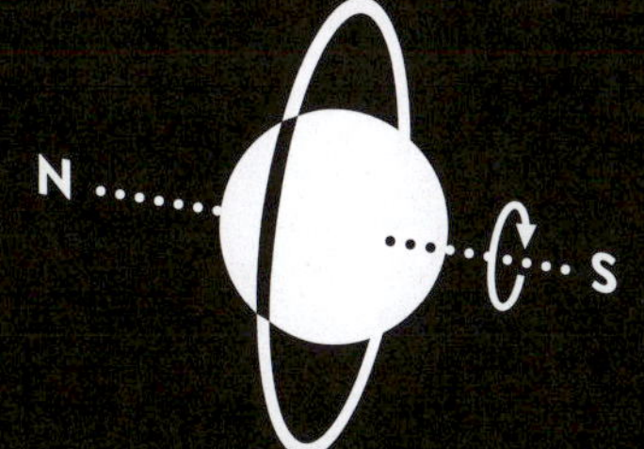

Rolling around

Something huge collided with Uranus billions of years ago, knocking the planet over on its side. And on its side is where Uranus has remained ever since – rolling around in space in its lopsided position.

Earth takes **365 days** to orbit the Sun, but it takes Uranus roughly **84 times longer** to make that same trip. Because of this, **1 year on Uranus** is equal to **84 Earth-years**, and each season lasts **21 years**. Uranus's peculiar orbit means that the Sun shines on the gas giant for the entire summer, but winter happens in total darkness. This means that a single day on the planet lasts for 21 years and a night lasts for another 21! On Uranus, you could be celebrating your **42nd birthday** and only have lived through a day and a night.

Scratch the surface

Not only would any spacecraft landing on Uranus be destroyed by the pressure and temperature, if they did manage to get to the surface there would be nowhere to land! Uranus is an ice giant from the outer solar system, and, because of this, it has no surface. Most of this wonderfully strange planet is made up of swirling fluids!

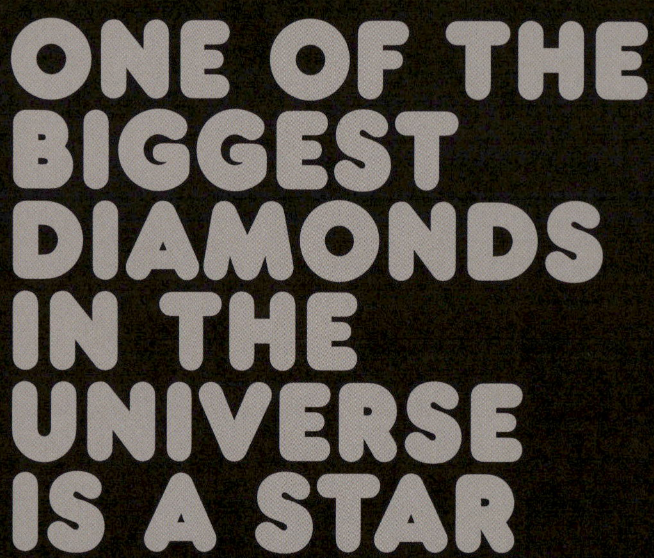

ONE OF THE BIGGEST DIAMONDS IN THE UNIVERSE IS A STAR

50 light-years away from Earth there's a pulsating diamond of **10 billion, trillion, trillion carats.** That is a 1 followed by 34 zeros! The diamond is actually the crystallized carbon interior of a white-dwarf star that ran out of nuclear fuel and died.

Twinkle twinkle

The largest diamond ever found on Earth doesn't even come close to its distant cosmic relative.

Name	Cullinan Diamond	BPM 37093
Nickname	Star of Africa	Lucy
Location	Earth	Centaurus constellation
Size	10.1 × 6.35 × 5.9 cm	7931 km diameter
Weight	621.35 g	2.188 x 10^30kg
Carats	3107	10 billion-trillion-trillion
Value	US$400,000,000	Priceless

Lucy

The dwarf star is officially called **BPM 37093**, but is more affectionately known as **Lucy**, after the Beatles' song 'Lucy in the Sky with Diamonds'.

Rock hard

Diamonds are the hardest natural substance we know of. The only material able to scratch a diamond is another diamond!

Cosmic gong

Not only does the star look stunning, but it sounds incredible too! Because of its constant pulsations, Lucy rings like a gigantic cosmic gong. Bongggggg!

Crystal ball

When we look at Lucy, we are likely seeing the future of the Sun. Scientists expect that, like BPM 37093, in **5 billion years'** time the Sun will go supernova, and in the **2 billion years** that follow it will crystallise into another glorious space diamond.

PLANETARY RAIN IS PRETTY CRAZY

When it starts to rain here on Earth, you can be pretty sure that it's only a form of water falling from the sky. But pulling out an umbrella on any other planet in the solar system won't be much use against what falls from those skies!

EARTH

The rain on Earth is actually **atmospheric water vapour** which has condensed into droplets of liquid water that become heavy enough to fall under the force of gravity.

SATURN

JUPITER

NEPTUNE

Scientists believe that it may rain tiny diamonds on Saturn, Jupiter and Neptune! It's speculated that floating carbon atoms could be pressurised through the super-thick atmospheres of these planet, creating tiny diamonds. But before the diamond rain reaches the surface, it's suspected that the high temperatures on these planets melt the sparkling rain it into an amazing diamond slush.

Sunshowers

Did you know it rains on the Sun? This rain is called **coronal rain** and occurs when hot plasma inside the Sun's outer atmosphere cools and condenses. This plasma then falls back to the Sun's surface because of the attraction of its magnetic field.

VENUS

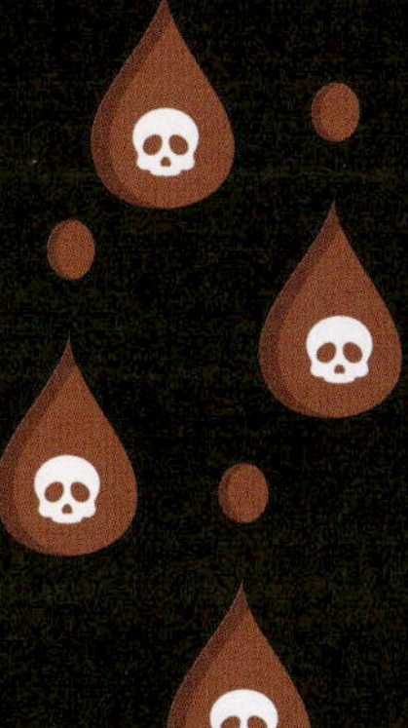

You'll definitely want to steer clear of the **sulphuric acid clouds** on Venus. Because the surface of the planet is so hot, these acid clouds turn to gas before they can even land on the surface of Venus.

TITAN

Titan is Saturn's largest moon and sits at a chilly **-179°C.** The low temperature on Titan causes **liquid methane rain** which has droplets twice as big as rain on Earth, falling at one fifth of the speed.

MARS

Scientists have found that Mars is the only planet in our solar system where it snows particles of carbon dioxide, more commonly called **dry ice**. The surface of Mars also sees the same snow we have on Earth, made from liquid water.

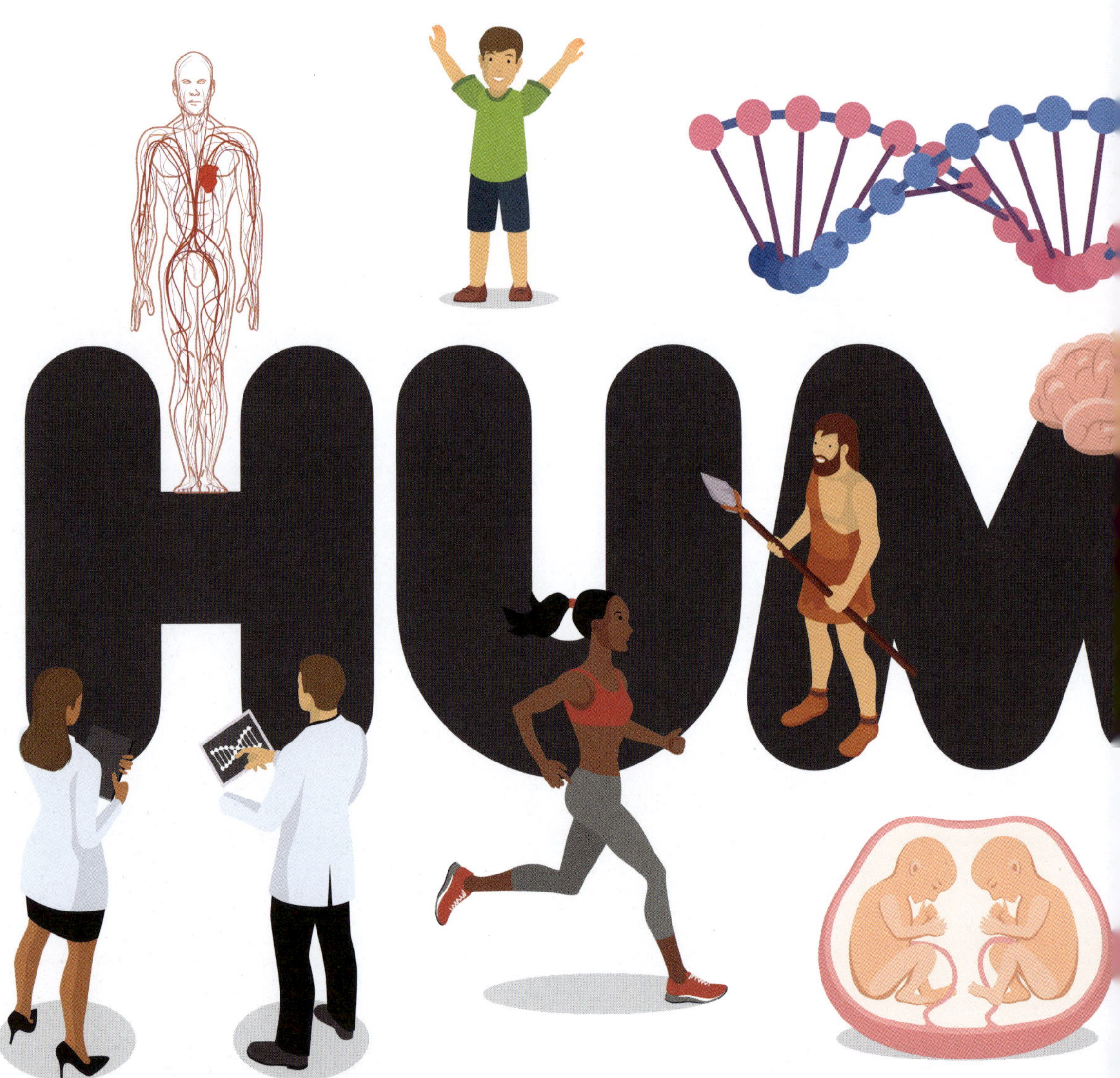
HUM

ANS

SOME PEOPLE CAN SEE SOUNDS AND HEAR COLOURS

Imagine if every time you heard a piano playing it felt like someone was massaging your scalp. Or if when you looked at a cat you tasted peanut butter. Or maybe Mondays are bright orange to you. All these things may sound completely wild, but they appear totally normal if you have a condition called **synaesthesia**.

Synaesthesia is a condition where your brain jumbles up your senses. It's usually inherited from your parents, but other than that the origins of the condition remain a mystery! People with synaesthesia often don't even realise that their experience of the world is very different until someone tells them that it is.

Seeing music

It's believed that Mozart had a form of synaesthesia, as he described musical keys in terms of colours. To him D major had a warm orange sound to it, while B-flat minor 'sounded' black. When writing his music, Mozart even used different colours to write different notes!

Super powers

Having synaesthesia is like having a superpower, and we all know that every superhero has a different power! There are several variations to synaesthesia, all with their own special traits.

Chromesthesia is where someone associates colours with sounds; they might hear a dog bark and it makes them think of the colour red. People with chromesthesia often have pitch-perfect hearing.

Those with **grapheme-colour synaesthesia** will see letters or numbers in certain colours. If they were to look at a page with a bunch of ones and twos jumbled together, they'd be able to pick out each number immediately, as they'd each appear in a separate colour.

People with **spatial-sequence synaesthesia** can see numerical sequences as points in space, which would be like seeing the year ahead as a three-dimensional map.

One of the most fascinating forms of synaesthesia is **mirror-touch synaesthesia**. This is where you can perceive someone else's feelings just by looking at them! It's no surprise that people with this (almost) mind-reading power have great empathy.

SYNAESTHESIA
0123456789

This is how someone with synaesthesia might see letters and numbers.

WE CAN OUR DRE...

Dreams within dreams

Have you ever woken up from a dream and gone about your day until something bizarre happens, making you realise you're still dreaming? This is called a **false awakening**. Everything before you wake the *second time* was actually still a dream. Some people even have dreams within dreams, and can experience many false awakenings before they really wake up.

ONTROL
MS

Do you sometimes realise you're dreaming while having a dream? If you do, then you've experienced a lucid dream! Lucid dreaming is when you know that you're dreaming, and are able to take control of the characters, storyline and even the environment.

Some people can even train themselves to have a lucid dream every night. Feel like flying? No problem at all, just take off and soar through the sky like a jet plane!

Humans spend a **third of their lives asleep** and about **6 years dreaming**. That's more than **2100 days** spent in a different world!

HUMANS CHALLENGE

Keep a dream diary by your bed and write in it as soon as you wake up before the memory fades away! What's the most exciting dream you can remember?

Render up

Everybody sleeps and everybody dreams, but not all of us can remember our dreams. The reason why we dream remains one of life's great mysteries. We know sleeping restores us to our best physical condition, but why we create detailed universes in our minds, complete with characters and stories, is still unknown.

Be in two minds

It's strange to think that your mind can both create a dream and then be surprised by what happens in it. Just like when you have a nightmare, your brain both creates the terror and then gets scared by it!

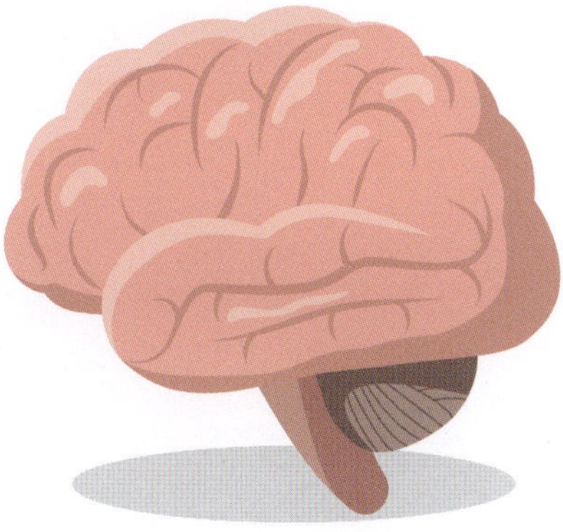

YOUR BRAIN IS LIKE A UNIVERSE

Your brain is the most amazing, astonishing and complex organ in the entire universe. It has around **86 billion neurons** – these are nerve cells which are responsible for sending messages through your whole body that communicate by sending chemical and electrical signals from your brain to your nerves.

100 TRILLION

That's the number of **synapses** your brain contains. Synapses are also known as the **neuronal junction** and are the place where your neurons communicate with one another.

Power up

A human brain has the ability to generate roughly **23 watts of power** when you're awake. That's just enough to power a light bulb!

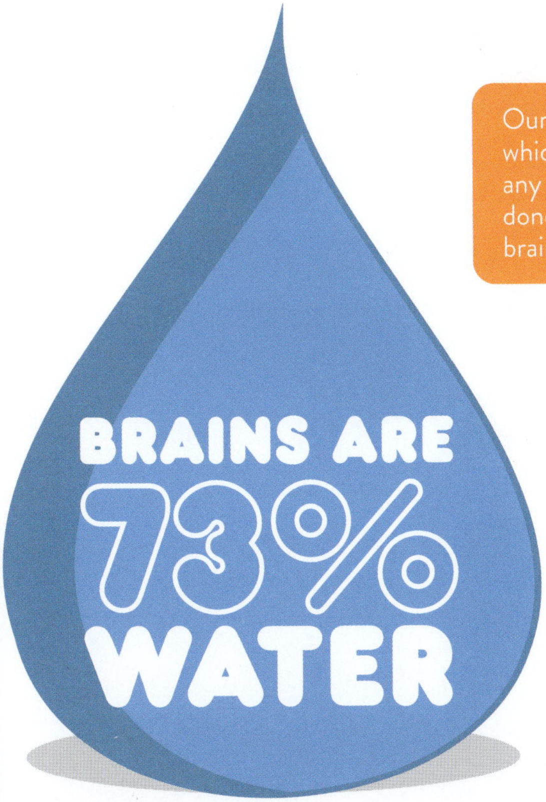

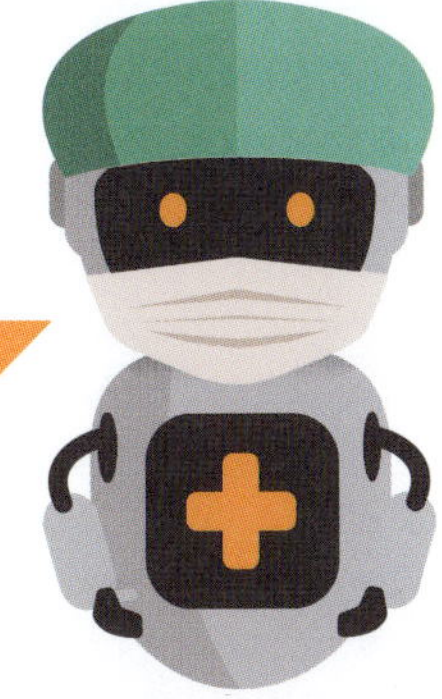

Our brains have no pain receptors, which means that they can't feel any pain. When people have surgery done on the brain technically the brain doesn't feel anything.

BRAINS ARE 73% WATER

431 KILOMETRES PER HOUR

This is the fastest speed that messages in our brain can travel. Messages in our brain can move faster than a Formula 1 car!

Take a sip

Drinking water is one of the best thing we can do for our bodies, especially our brains. What happens to your brain when you become dehydrated is pretty scary: your attention and your memory are affected, as well as your ability to do the simplest of tasks – never mind complicated ones.

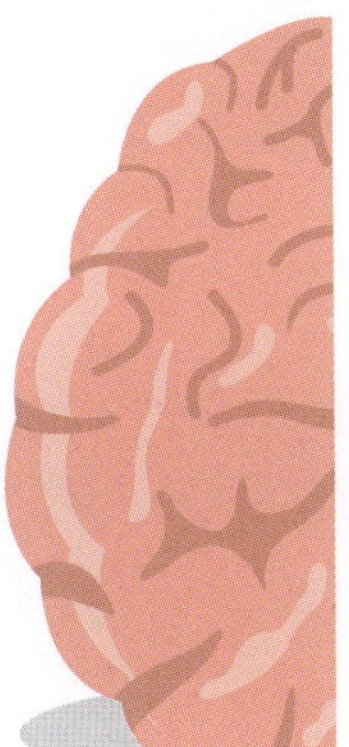

Not half bad

A **hemispherectomy** is when half of a brain is surgically removed or disabled for the treatment of seizures. This procedure can take place with no adverse effects on the patient's personality, memory or sense of humour!

Rocket science

Scientific research and discovery can often require a **control group** and a **test group**. Sets of twins are the perfect control and test subjects, as they share so many attributes. In fact, scientists once sent a twin to the International Space Station (ISS) for **340 days** to monitor how his body changed compared to his twin brother back on Earth. Among the findings were a big difference in gene activity for the twin in space, the development of thicker skin on his forehead and a slightly different eyeball shape.

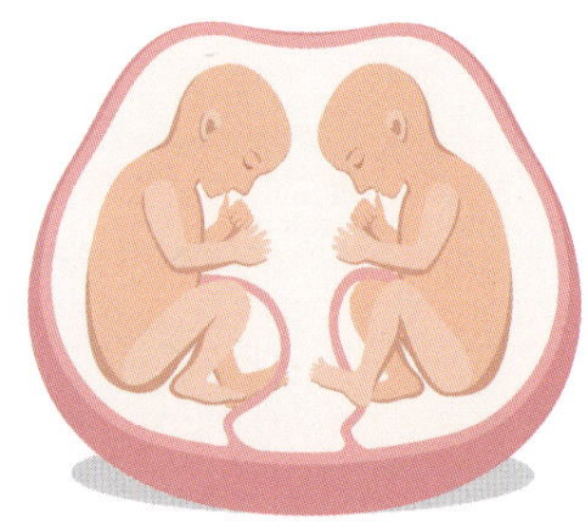

Social network

Twins first interact with one another inside their mother's womb. They've even been observed stroking the head and back of their sibling in utero.

Out of print

Although identical twins share the same genetics, they do not share the same fingerprints. However, their identical genes do give them similar patterns.

Double talk

Cryptophasia is a phenomenon where twins create a unique language to communicate with each other, usually as children. This secret language cannot be understood by anyone else!

... ARE AS SIMILAR AS IDENTICAL TWINS WHO GROW UP TOGETHER

When scientists studied more than **100 sets of identical twins** who grew up apart, results showed that although they weren't raised together, they were still incredibly alike. These twins all had similar personalities, attitudes, temperaments and interests!

WE ARE ALL MUTANTS

Blueprint

Deoxyribonucleic acid (or **DNA** if you can't attempt that tongue-twister) is the building block of life. It's made up of two long molecules arranged in a spiral, like a twisted ladder, and is commonly referred to as the **double-helix structure**.

DNA is present in the nucleus of every single cell in your body. It carries genetic information and has the instructions that any given living organism needs to grow, reproduce and function. Don't leave home without it.

Mutants aren't always the comic-book superheros or terrifying monsters we see in movies. A mutation is simply a change in an organism's genetic material, and they happen in our bodies every day. We're all mutants!

Mutations are changes that happen by mistake, and in our case the material that is changing is our DNA. Mutations can occur when our DNA is being copied, or sometimes due to exposure to chemicals or radiation. Without mutation, life on Earth would still be the layer of slime that it was **3.6 billion years ago**. Life stayed in slime-form for **1 billion years**, until mutations began occurring and evolution exploded into action; this changed our DNA through history and led all the way up to you reading this book today!

Don't stop me now

Humans have been mutating throughout history and will continue to do so in the future, although the speed at which these mutations occur is slowing down. There are now fewer new mutations in humans per year than in our closest animal relatives, the chimpanzee.

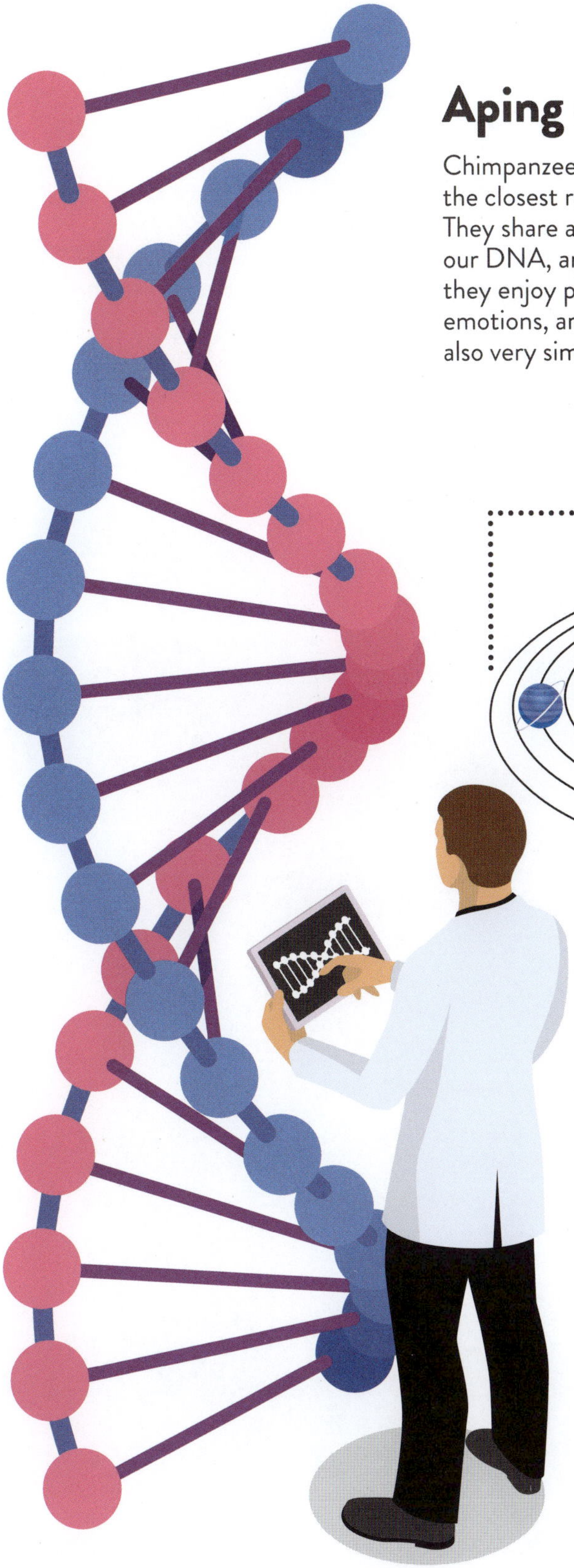

Aping around

Chimpanzees are genetically the closest relative of humans. They share almost **99%** of our DNA, and just like us they enjoy playing around, have emotions, are intelligent and are also very similar to us physically.

Diameter: 10 billion km

Laid out

If you laid out all the DNA molecules in your body end to end, they would span the diameter of the solar system, twice! There's a whopping **20 billion kilometres** of DNA inside you!

Know different

Each human is **99.9%** genetically the same as every other human on the planet. That teeny tiny **0.1%** difference in our genes determines everything from what eye colour we have to whether we are likely to get a certain disease when we're older.

WE ARE ATOMS THAT PONDER OTHER ATOMS

Everything in the universe is made up of atoms, from the stars in the night sky to the ground at your feet – and your feet as well! Atoms are the foundation of our world. They are very, very, very small and are made up of even tinier particles. You're actually just one big collection of atoms that spends their time thinking about other collections of atoms.

Spinning around

Electron is the smallest of the three particles, and has a negative charge

Neutron has no electric charge

Proton has a positive electric charge

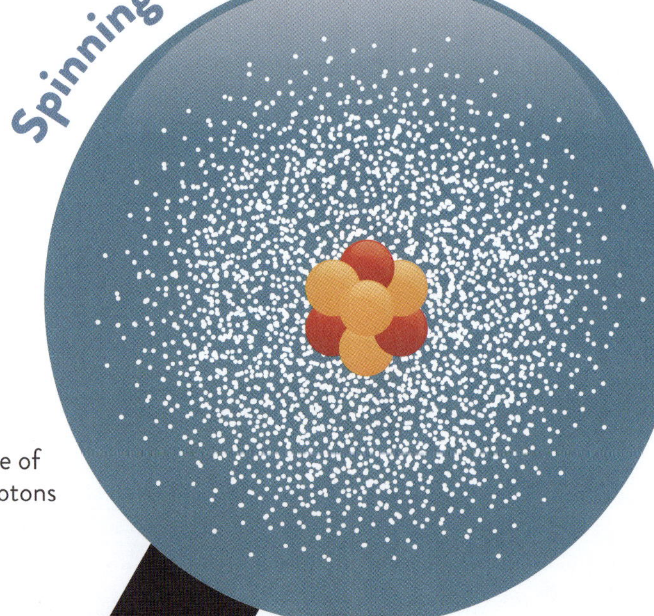

The nucleus lives at the centre of an atom and is made up of protons and neutrons. The electrons spin in orbit around the shell that surrounds the nucleus.

Octilions

As the atoms in our body are so tiny it takes a lot of them to actually make a person. An adult is made up of around **7,000,000,000,000, 000,000,000,000,000** atoms, or **7 octillion atoms**!

Body of water

About **99%** of your body is made up of hydrogen, carbon, nitrogen and oxygen atoms. Up to **60%** of an adult human's body is made of water, which is just hydrogen and oxygen atoms.

Running on empty

An atom's nucleus is around **100,000 times smaller** than the atom it lives in. If you imagined an atom to be the size of a football stadium, then the nucleus would be a tiny mosquito in the centre of the pitch! The size difference between the atom and the nucleus leaves a lot of space inside. If we lost all that dead space in our atoms, we'd be able to fit the entire human race inside a single sugar cube!

COMMON AS

Hydrogen is the most common atom in the universe. Almost three quarters of the atoms in the Milky Way galaxy are hydrogen atoms!

785 m

EVERY HUMAN ON EARTH COULD FIT IN A 785-METRE -SIDED BOX

As large as life

There's already an incredible number of humans calling Earth home, but every year there are more and more. The world's population is growing by **1.10%** per year, that's roughly **83 million** more people annually. The global population is expected to reach **8.6 billion in 2030**, **9.8 billion in 2050** and **11.2 billion in 2100**. Talk about jam packed.

What would happen if all **7.8 billion humans** decided to live together as one giant family, just how big would our home have to be? Surprisingly, we could all fit inside a building just over 785 metres wide and the same height and depth. On the downside, our new home would have no windows and we would all be packed in as closely as possible. It would be a pretty awful experience, but our home wouldn't take up much more than a few blocks in any of the world's major cities!

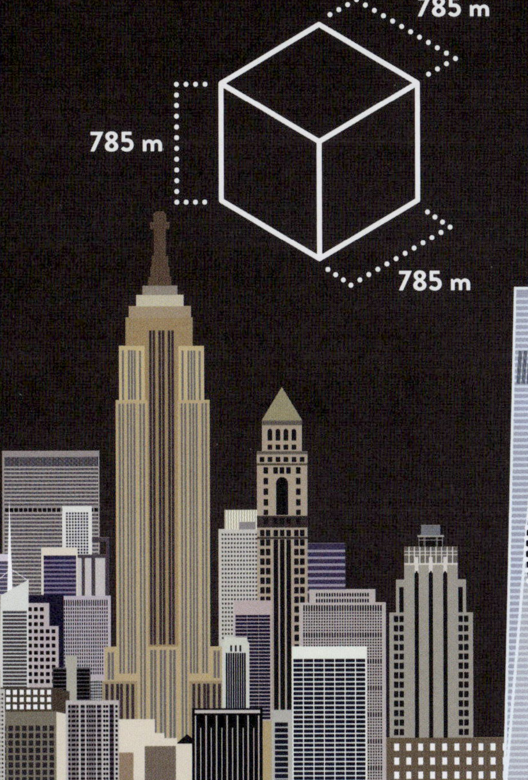

0.062 cubic metres is the average physical space taken up by a human body.

Number cruncher

We know that there are **7,800,000,000 people** in the world and that, on average, they each take up **0.062 cubic metres**. When we multiply these numbers together it gives us the total space taken up by all humans, which is **483,600,000 cubic metres**.

If we want to find out what width of cube can produce this number of cubic metres, we find the cube root ($\sqrt[3]{}$) of **483,600,000**, which equals **784.9 metres**. Ta dah!

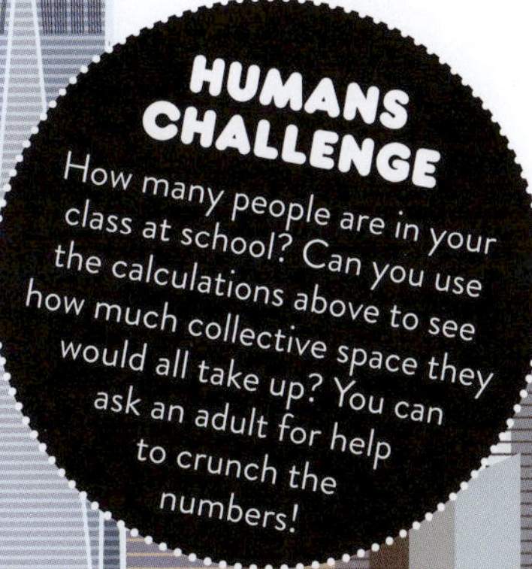

WE HAVE MORE THAN FIVE SENSES

Your senses are how your body discovers and understands the world around it. We all know the traditional five senses: **touch**, **sight**, **taste**, **hearing** and **smell**. But these five are just the beginning. Our incredible bodies may actually have more than twenty senses including **hunger**, **thirst** and **knowing when to go to the toilet**. In order for us to have senses, we need **sensors** to detect them. Sensors include our **eyes**, **ears**, **nose**, **skin** and **tongue**. Not to mention the other sensors, like our **blood**, **bladder** and **large intestine**!

There are **sensors** in your muscles and joints that tell you where your body parts are in relation to one another. These sensors are what allow us to touch our fingertips together or touch our noses with our eyes shut. Go ahead, close your eyes and try it now!

Eyes: Your eyes have two different types of light sensors: **rod cells** and **cone cells**. Our rod cells are used to sense light intensity, and they respond when you are in low light. There are also three cone cells which sense each of the primary colours (red, green and blue). These cone cells require bright light to sense colour.

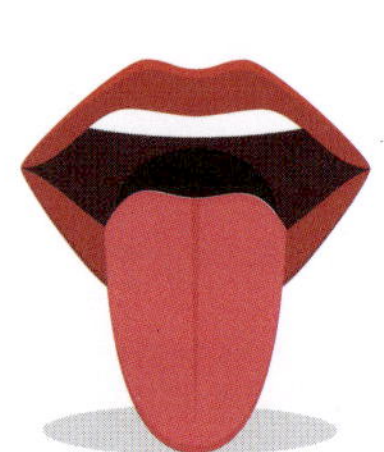

Tongue: Your tongue contains chemical receptors that give you a sense of taste. Yum, yum!

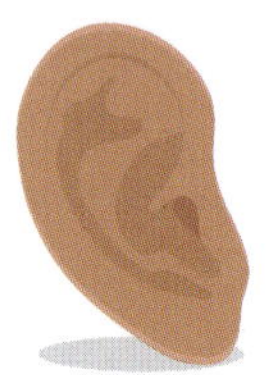

Ears: There are sound sensors in your inner ear that respond to vibrating soundwaves, as well as sensors that detect your position in the Earth's gravitational field to give you a sense of balance!

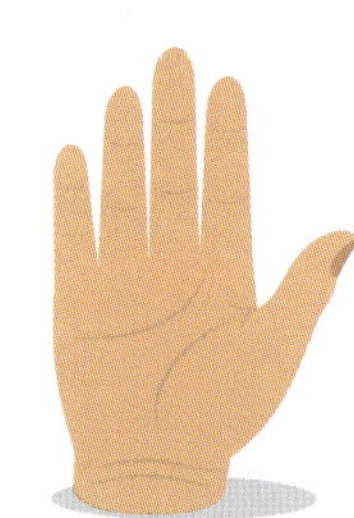

Skin: Your skin is an amazing sensor, and a busy one too! Your sense of touch, pain, temperature and itchiness are all thanks to at least five different types of nerve endings that live beneath your skin.

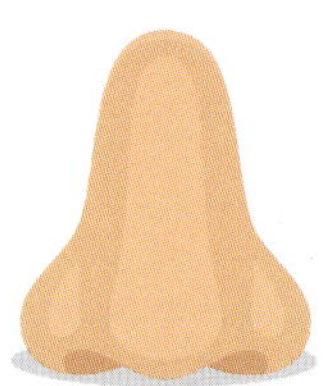

Nose: Inside your nose there are hundreds of different chemical sensors that give you a sense of smell.

Blood: There are chemical sensors in your blood that check salt and glucose levels, and these sensors are how your body knows to tell you when you're hungry and thirsty.

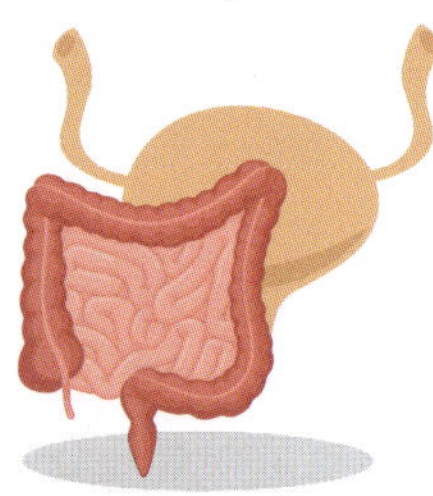

Bladder and intestines: The reason you know when it's time to go to the toilet is because of the sensors inside your bladder and large intestine.

Sixth sense

There are some people who claim to have other special senses too, such as feeling like they know when someone is looking at them or being able to tell when a weather change is coming. Do you have a special sixth sense?

HUMANS CHALLENGE

See if you can test out how contagious yawns actually are by pretending to yawn in front of ten different people. How many yawned back?

IT'S A MYSTERY WHY WE YAWN

A good yawn is often associated with feeling tired or waking up from a good night's sleep. But humans also yawn when they're bored, anxious, hungry or about to do something new! Did you know that yawns are contagious? Next time you see someone yawn, try to stop yourself from yawning too! Even just reading about yawning makes people yawn. In fact, I bet you are yawning right now! We know a lot about when we yawn, but the exact reason *why* we yawn remains a mystery.

Breathe it in

Just what exactly *is* a yawn? A scientist would describe it as an action in which someone opens and stretches their mouth and throat, and then breathes air in and out. After doing so they immediately close their mouth. Often this yawn is just the first of a series, as people will generally yawn for a second and a third time (sometimes even more). Stopping a good yawning session can be quite hard!

6 SECONDS

This is the average length of a yawn, but men generally yawn longer than women. During that brief **6 seconds**, your heart rate can increase by as much as **30%**.

Everybody yawns

It would appear that everybody yawns, even unborn babies in the womb! Cats, dogs, birds and fish have all been known to yawn as well. Dogs usually have a great big yawn when they see their owners, and sometimes hearing their owner yawn may cause a dog to do the same!

Spare your blushes

Lots of animals yawn, but only humans blush. This usually happens when you're in a stressful situation or feeling embarrassed. Your skin looks redder and feels hotter, especially your cheeks. But did you know that you're blushing on the inside too? When you blush, your body is producing adrenaline which causes you to breathe more quickly, your heart to beat faster and your blood vessels to widen. This process increases the blood flow to your stomach lining, causing it to blush!

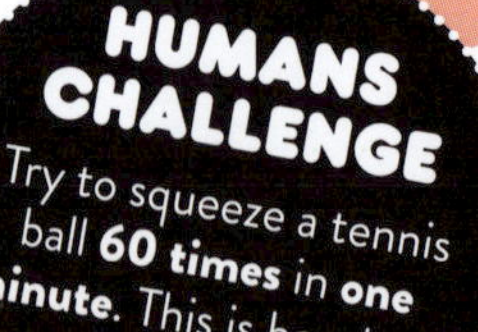

YOUR HEART WILL BEAT MORE THAN THREE BILLION TIMES IN YOUR LIFE

You have lots and lots of muscles in your body, but your hard-working heart is the most important of all. The heart just keeps going and going, pumping oxygen-rich blood all around your body, and it does this without you even having to think about it!

When resting, the heart will beat around **60** to **100 times per minute**. During exercise, your heart beats on average **80 times per minute**, which is **4800** beats per hour. In a day, your heart is likely to beat close to **115,200 times**. Over a whole year that is **42,048,000 beats**! So, if you lived to be **80 years old**, your heart would have beat approximately **3,363,840,000 times**!

150,000

That's the total length in kilometres of all the blood vessels in your body. If all your arteries, veins and capillaries were laid out in a line, they would be long enough to stretch around the world almost **four times**!

7500

The number of litres of blood your heart can pump around your body daily, supplying your organs and tissues with the oxygen and nutrients you need to stay alive.

75 TRILLION

That's the number of cells in your body that receive blood from your heart. The clear protective outer layer of your eye, the cornea, is the only place that receives no blood supply.

A tennis ball can show you just how hard your heart works. The amount of force you use to squeeze a tennis ball with one hand is the same amount required for your heart to contract and push blood through your body.

Beat it

Your heart has its own electrical impulse. This impulse means that if your heart was ever separated from your body it would continue to beat as long as it had a suitable supply of oxygen.

Sweet harmony

Harmonising their voices is not the only thing that choirs synchronise; these singers also harmonise their heartbeats! When a choir sings together, their pulses speed up and slow down at the same rate, quickly becoming synchronised and beating in the same rhythm.

HUMANS CAN OUT

RUN ANY ANIMAL

Although it might not feel like it when you're puffing and panting, you were actually born to run! Humans have evolved to be able to run better than any animal on this planet when it comes to endurance running. Humans can outrun horses, lions and even the fastest land animal in the world, the cheetah. We may not be the fastest (having only two legs is always a disadvantage against our four-legged friends), but we can go the distance!

For nearly **40 years** the Welsh town of Llanwrtyd Wells has held its annual **35 kilometres man-versus-horse race**. Regular people often beat many of the competing horses, especially on the hotter days when the humans can expel the heat better.

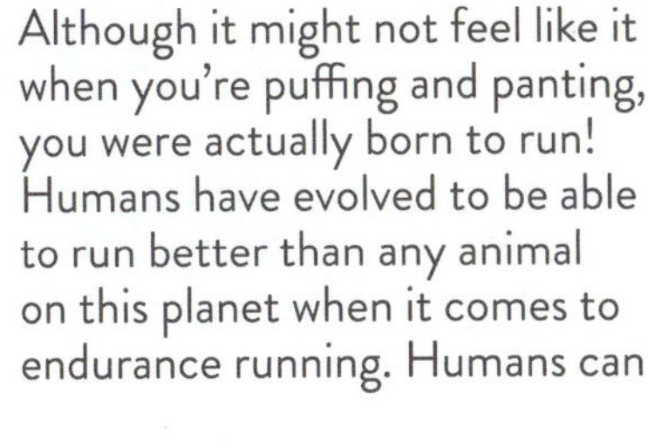

Sweat it out

So how did we become such epic endurance runners? It's because of our sweat! Humans have **2–4 million** sweat glands covering our body, which allow us to cool ourselves while we're running. Not being covered head to toe in thick hair is also a massive advantage!

Just run with it

Our ancestors developed the ability to run in order to hunt faster prey, like antelopes and gazelles. Over time we have developed an evolutionary edge which has allow us to track prey over long distances, until it either overheated or was manoeuvred into a trap. Dinnertime!

HUMANS ARE ADAPTING TO LIFE UNDER THE WATER

We humans tend to live above the water on land, and when you hold your breath underwater, it's not hard to understand why. But the challenging experience of holding your breath isn't the same for every human; there are some of us who are adapting to a life spent underwater. The **Bajau people** of **Southeast Asia** are able to lower their heartbeat to a mere **30 beats per minute** as they comfortably drop to **70 metres** depth and stay below the surface for up to **13 minutes** while they hunt for food. The Bajau people can often spend up to **60%** of their workdays under the water! They've even evolved to have bigger spleens, an organ which makes more oxygen available in their blood, lessening their need to breathe while underwater.

24 MINUTES

This is the longest a human has held their breath underwater. This feat was oxygen assisted, which means it was achieved by breathing pure oxygen from a tank and filling the lungs to capacity before going underwater.

Dive in

Strangely enough, humans are all able to hold their breath longer underwater than we can on land. As soon as we're submerged our bodies activate something called the **diving response**. This is where your heart rate slows, your blood vessels shrink and your spleen contracts. All of these responses are designed to save energy when you're low on oxygen.

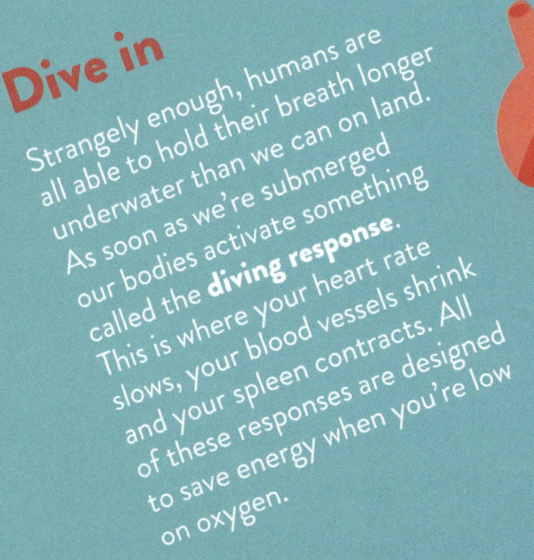

Tyred out

If you've ever been in a bath or the pool for long enough, you'll have noticed that the skin on your fingers and toes shrivels up like an old prune. It's believed that the reason for these wrinkly fingers and toes is that the wrinkles channel away the water, much like the tread of a car tyre, and improve our grip on wet objects when we're submerged.

YOUR MIND CAN CURE YOUR BODY

When you're feeling unwell and go to the doctor, they will often prescribe medicine to help you get better. This may be how medicine usually works, but have you heard of the **placebo effect**? Sometimes, instead of giving real medicine, doctors can provide people with fake medicine without them knowing. But don't worry, doctors only do this in certain circumstances and after lots of research. Many of these people see real improvement in their conditions; however, everyone responds differently. The false medicine is called a **placebo**, which is why we call this the **placebo effect**. It's believed that the improvement comes from a patient's expectation that the placebo will help them. It seems that the greater the belief you have that the treatment is going to help you, the greater the chance you'll experience a positive change.

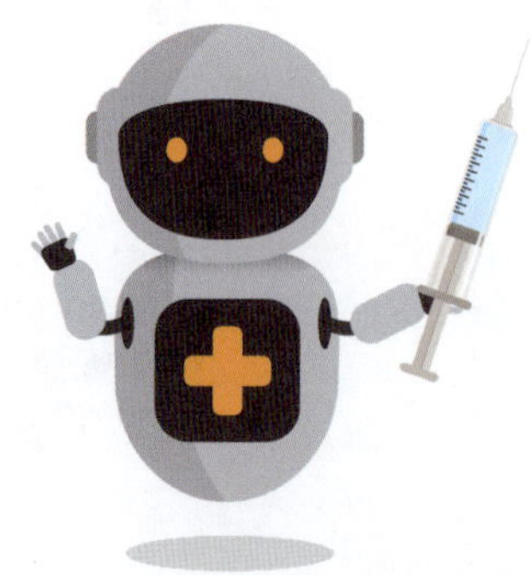

With pleasure

Placebos work best if you are in physical pain. This is because they can cause your brain to release hormones called **endorphins** and **dopamine**, which reduce your pain and increase feelings of pleasure, as well as relaxing you.

Made to measure

Rather than trying to fool you, doctors use placebos to help them better understand what effect a new drug or treatment might have on a medical condition. Placebos are often used in **clinical trials**, where some groups are given a placebo and others are given the new drug. The effects of the placebo and new drug are then measured and compared to help doctors better understand the effect of the active drugs and the placebos themselves.

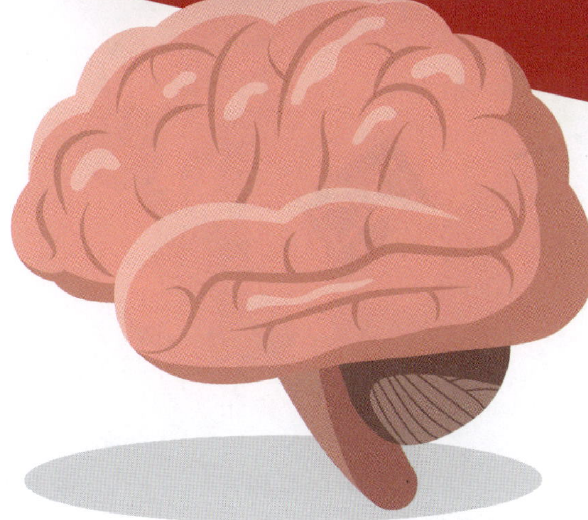

Mind over matter

Scientists cannot determine how the placebo effect works, only what it reveals. The placebo effect shows that our minds have far more control over what happens in our bodies than we may like to think.

Sweet as sugar

Placebos often come as an inactive substance like a sugar pill, saline solution or distilled water.

HUMANS GLOW IN THE DARK

Fireflies, jellyfish, glow-worms and those terrifying deep-sea creatures that look like they're from another planet are just some of the famous light-emitting beings that live on Earth. But did you know that almost all living creatures emit a very weak light, including you! You're glowing right now, and while this may be a very faint glow, it is most definitely still a glow!

Inside our bodies, there are chemical reactions occurring that free energy and produce heat. These chemicals reactions also create small numbers of **photons**, which are the **elementary particles of light**. Because of this reaction, your body is emitting a small glow, and the intensity of that glow rises and falls as the day goes by. Your glow is at its strongest in the late afternoon, and brightest around the lower part of your face. Unfortunately, we're not able to see our glow, as it is **1000 times** less intense than the level of light that your eyes can detect. However, scientists are able to use a special, sensitive camera to see our glow!

Say cheese

The camera required to capture your glow is super sensitive. It can detect light at the level of a single photon and needs to operate in a completely light-tight room at **-120°C**. The person being filmed also needs to be clean, naked and in complete darkness. That's one tough photoshoot!

Good afternoon

Your body's glow will change at different times of the day. The lowest glow-point is at **10 am**, and the peak at **4 pm**. After the peak, our glow gradually drops off again, which is likely because our glow is linked to our body's clock and rhythms.

Face value

Your face, particularly your mouth and cheeks, glows more than the rest of the body. Scientists suspect that this could be because our faces have more exposure to sunlight, and therefore tend to be more tanned than the rest of the body. **Melanin**, the pigment behind your skin colour, has fluorescent components that could be enhancing your body's tiny glow.

ONLY A THIRD OF THE POPULATION CAN DRINK MILK

If you enjoy a nice cold glass of milk with your cookies, then you're very lucky, as two thirds of all humans are unable to stomach dairy! Being unable to drink milk and eat dairy products means that you're **lactose intolerant**, which is when you can't digest the main sugar found in milk – **lactose**. Most people stop being able to digest this sugar between the ages of 2 and 5 and if they try, the results are pretty horrible; producing gas that can cause farting, bloating, cramps and diarrhea. But if two thirds of the world are lactose intolerant, perhaps we should stop calling this a disease and assume that drinking milk is not normal!

Milking it

People living in Sweden and Finland have super-high tolerance levels for lactose. The Swedes are **74%** tolerant to dairy, and the Finns are **82%** tolerant!

A world of difference

There are pretty big differences between countries and regions where lactose intolerance is most prevalent. In Northern Europe, the rates can be as low as **5%**, whereas in Asia the rates can be as high as **90%**. It is estimated that **40 million people** in America suffer from some form of lactose intolerance!

Rough rates of lactose intolerance in different regions of the world

OUR BRAIN IS IGNORING OUR NOSE

If you look at your face in the mirror, one of the first things you'll notice is your nose. Proud as punch, sitting in the centre of your face, your nose is one of your most notable facial features. And yet, when we turn away from the mirror, we no longer see our noses – even though they're right there in our field of vision!

Our noses are missing because our brains are ignoring them. Brains cleverly filter your nose out of your vision, as seeing your nose constantly is not needed for you to get on with your life. There is nothing to be gained by having a constant visual reminder that you have a nose!

Eye eye

Your nose blocks out some of the visual field of both your eyes. Your brain takes information from what you can see through the unblocked portion of your eye and builds a complete picture from there. Genius!

On the side

Another reason why you don't notice your nose is because it's in your side vision, as well as being very close to your eyes, which makes your nose out of focus as you look at things which are further away.

Look past

It isn't just your nose that your brain is filtering out; there's a whole heap of other visual information that's removed for you too. For instance, if you wear glasses you probably don't even notice you're wearing them! If your brain didn't filter this unnecessary information, you would become overwhelmed with sensory input.

HUMANS CHALLENGE

You can see your nose right now. Close one eye and your nose will instantly appear on the side where your eye is open. Now close the other eye and the same thing happens on your other side! When you open both your eyes again your nose will instantly vanish. Ta dah!

THERE ARE GERMS IN YOUR GUT ...

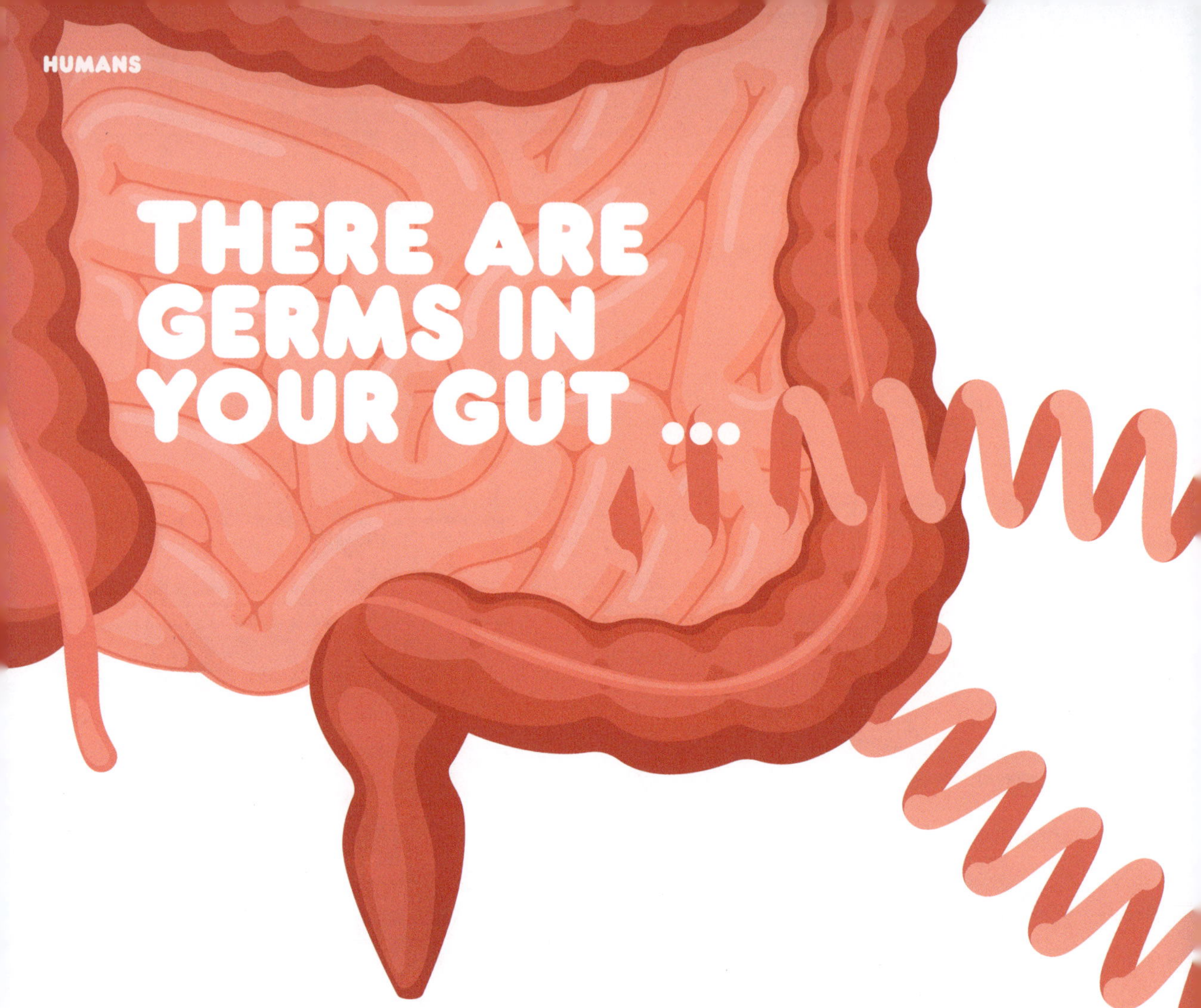

Even when you're by yourself, you're never really alone. It may sound freaky, but the inside and outside of your body are home to **trillions of bacteria**, **viruses**, **fungi** and other tiny living organisms called **microbes**. There are so many of these tiny creatures living inside us that they actually outnumber our own human cells!

These microscopic creatures play a huge role in your wellbeing, helping your immune system, providing nutrients for your cells and preventing invasions from other harmful bacteria and viruses. Almost all of these tiny creatures call your gut their home, and it is from here that they communicate directly with your brain. We still don't know exactly what they're saying, but whatever it is influences your brain, affecting your behaviour and mental health. No way!

TRILLION

This is the number of microbes living inside your gut!

200G

The total weight of all the microbes that call your gut home.

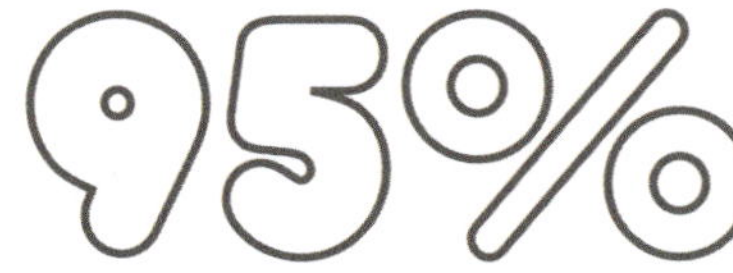

This is the percentage of microbiome that live in your gut, which extends from your mouth all the way down to your bottom.

Brain box

As well as providing a home to all those amazing microbes, your gut acts like a second brain and can think for itself thanks to the **100 million neurons** inside it. It immediately digests food without your brain telling it to. None of your other organs, not even your super-powerful heart, can do that.

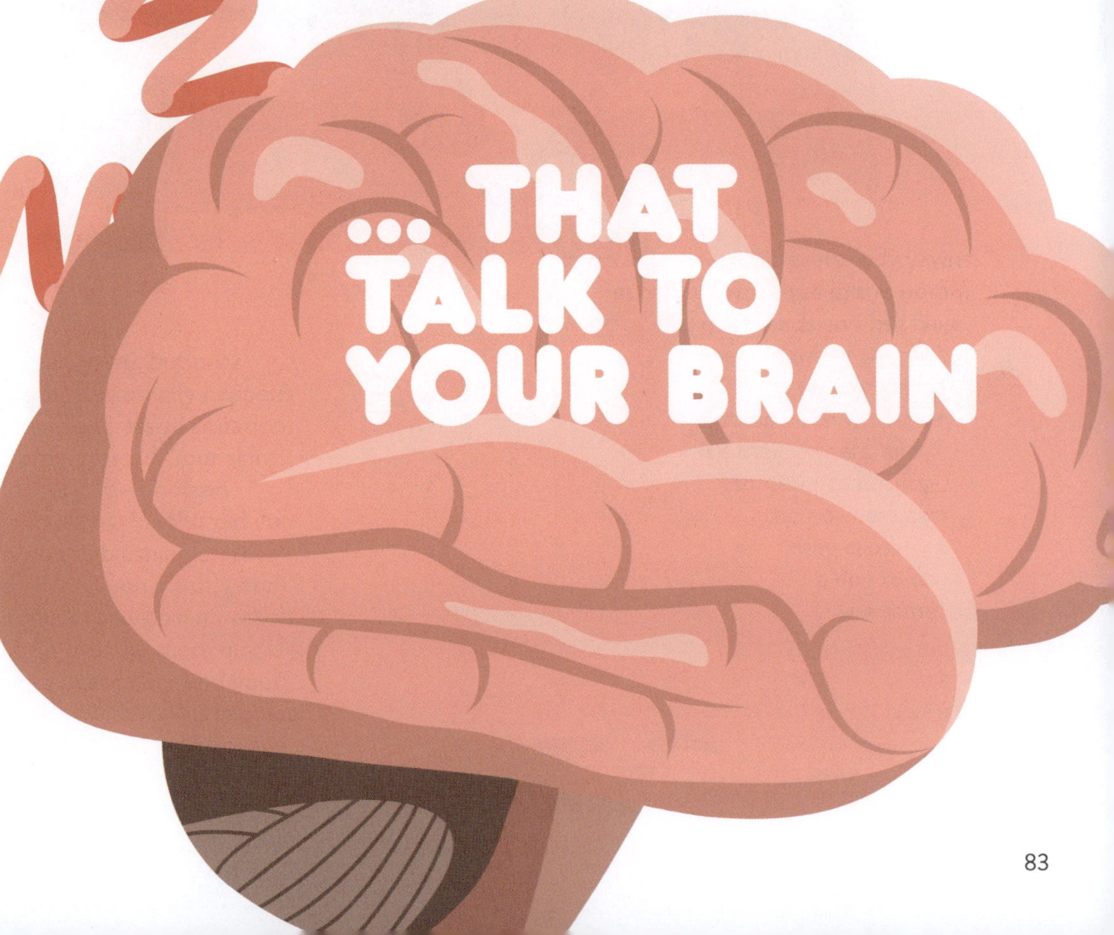

Curly wurly

Our intestines have a surface area of around **32 square metres**, and they're all curled up inside us. That's the same size as a small apartment!

Mice and men

Scientists first discovered the connection between your gut microbiome and your brain with studies conducted mainly on mice. Scientists continue to conduct studies using our furry friends to this day.

... THAT TALK TO YOUR BRAIN

EARTH IS SLOWING DOWN

Our planet is constantly spinning. If you ever need to check this is true, just look and see the Sun as it changes position in the sky – the Sun is actually staying put and it's us that's moving! Earth is constantly spinning on its axis, completing a full rotation every **23 hours** and **56 minutes**. Amazingly, the inhabitants of Earth (us included) aren't able to feel this spinning at all because everything around us (including the Earth's atmosphere) is rotating too! If Earth ever suddenly slammed on the cosmic brakes, we'd know about it pretty quickly as the atmosphere would keep travelling at its original speed, wiping the surface of the planet clean in the process.

All this information makes the fact that Earth is slowing down a little worrying. But there's no need to panic, the deceleration is only tiny, and that's all thanks to the Moon and its pull on our tides. Roughly every **100 years**, the day gets about **1.4 milliseconds** (or **1.4 thousandths of a second**) longer. No need to go changing your clocks just yet!

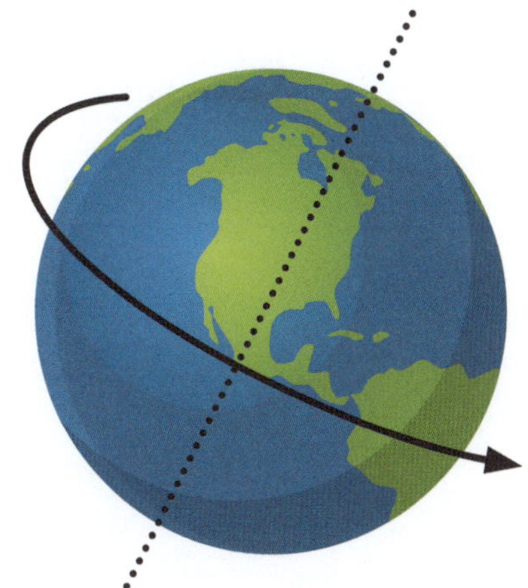

1670 KILOMETRES PER HOUR

The speed of the Earth's rotation at the equator.

107,226 KILOMETRES PER HOUR

Earth's speed as it orbits the Sun.

Although they're staying put relative to Earth's orbit, both the Sun and the solar system are actually moving at **720,000 kilometres per hour** as they travel around the centre of the Milky Way galaxy. But even at this incredible speed it is still going to take about **230 million years** to travel all the way around the galaxy. That's a long road trip!

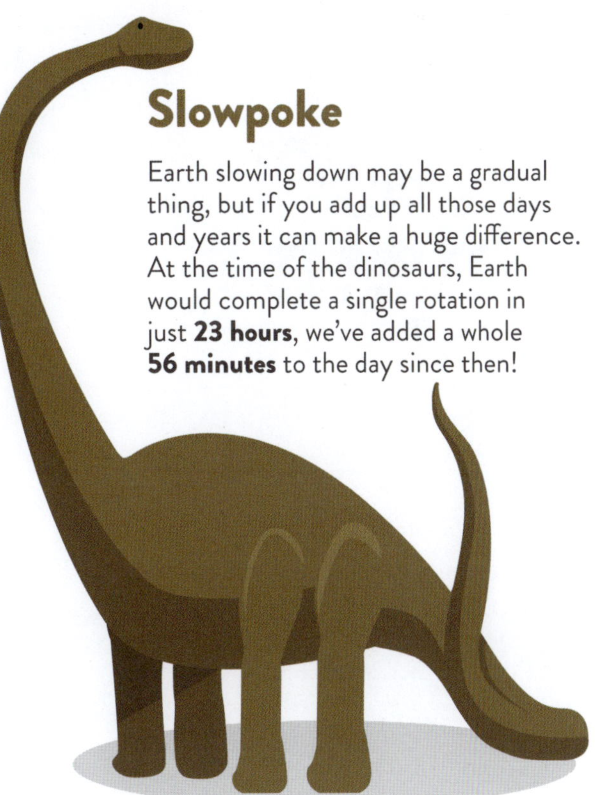

Slowpoke

Earth slowing down may be a gradual thing, but if you add up all those days and years it can make a huge difference. At the time of the dinosaurs, Earth would complete a single rotation in just **23 hours**, we've added a whole **56 minutes** to the day since then!

Lumps and bumps

Aside from the flat poles and bulge in the middle, Earth is pretty lumpy and bumpy! The Moon's gravity plays a part in warping the shape of the Earth by distorting the continents and oceans.

Earth is very, very old, but calculating just how old Earth is has proved quite tricky – there's no birth certificate for a planet, after all! To figure out the Earth's age, scientists have dated the rocks of the Earth's crust, as well as rocks from the Moon and various meteorites that have landed on Earth. From this, they've calculated the Earth's age to be **4.543 billion years**.

THE EARTH IS NOT ROUND

Yes, you did read that correctly, the Earth is not perfectly round. But that doesn't mean it's flat either. In fact, the Earth is actually an **oblate spheroid**, which is a fancy way of saying that it flattens at the poles and then widens out at the equator. It's very close to, but not exactly, a perfect sphere.

Earth is shaped like this because it's rotating. The planet bulges at the equator because of **centrifugal force** during rotation, just like when someone makes a pizza base by spinning it. The mass pushes outwards and flattens out along the axis of rotation.

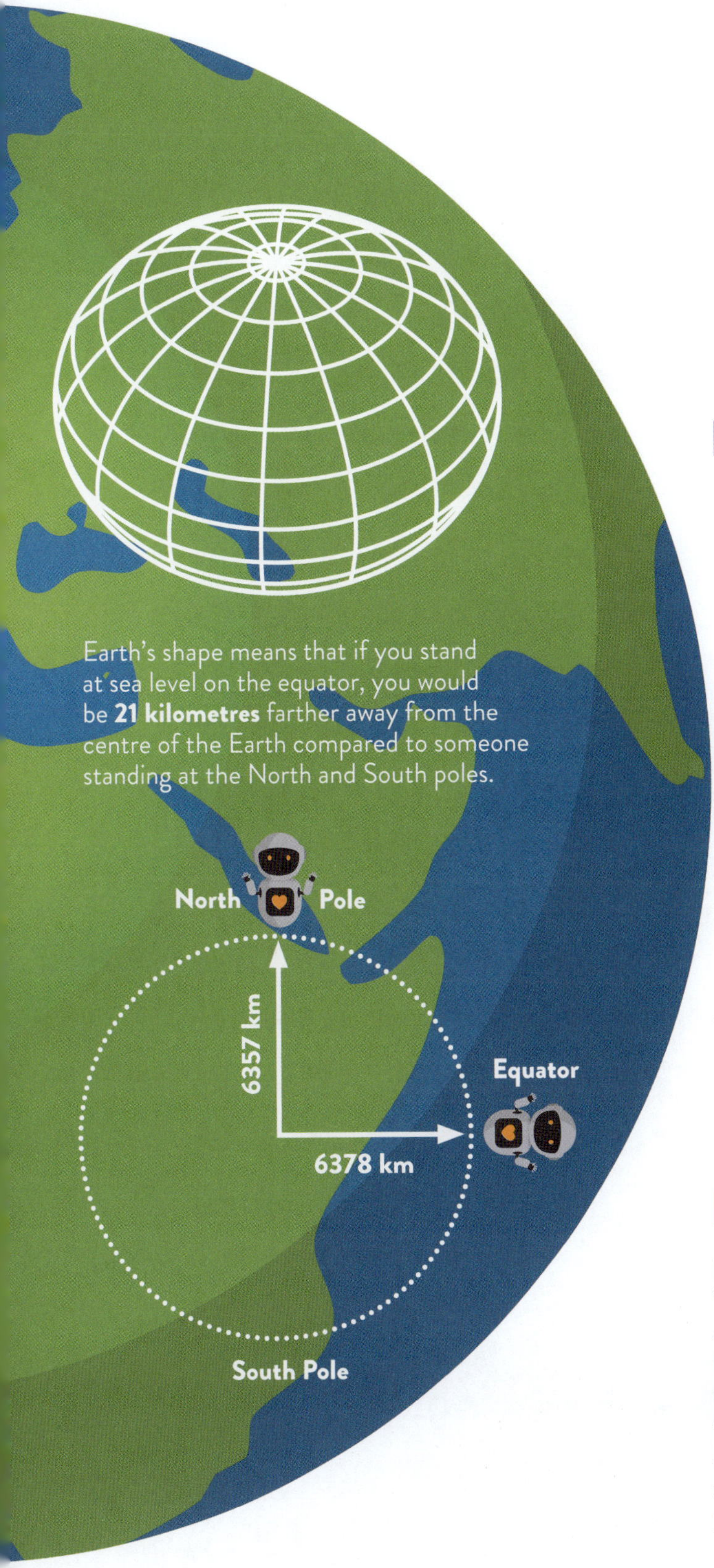

Earth's shape means that if you stand at sea level on the equator, you would be **21 kilometres** farther away from the centre of the Earth compared to someone standing at the North and South poles.

North Pole

6357 km

Equator

6378 km

South Pole

Purple patch

Earth, as we recognise it today, is blue and green. But scientists think that millions of years ago the planet may have been a vibrant purple! It's thought that ancient microbes may have used a different method to obtain energy from the Sun, which would have made the planet appear violet.

Name of the game

Nobody knows who named Earth. What we do know is that the name comes from a combination of the English word **'eor(th)e/ertha'** and the German word **'erde'**, both of which mean **'ground'**. Earth is also the only planet in our solar system that isn't named after a Greek or Roman god or goddess.

THERE ARE THREE TRILLION TREES ON EARTH

You don't have to look very far to see a tree or two. They're everywhere, even in the most unexpected places like big cities. All of the trees we see every day are actually part of a huge family of 3 trillion – **3.041 trillion** trees. This means that for every human living on Earth there are over **400 trees**! Trees aren't just there to look pretty, though. They work extremely hard to filter water, battle air pollution and remove vast amounts of carbon from our atmosphere. In addition to all this hard work, trees provide permanent shelter for many different animals including insects, arachnids, amphibians, reptiles, birds and mammals. As a species, trees have called Earth home for **370 million years** and some are several thousand years old themselves! Nothing on Earth lives as long as a tree.

A tall tale

Earth is **4.5 billion years old**, but for the first **90%** of its life trees weren't even around! Instead of trees, there were enormous fungi that grew to an enormous **8 metres** in height!

THE OLDEST TREE IS 9550 YEARS OLD

Sweden is home to the world's oldest tree. A **Norwegian Spruce** named **Old Tjikko**. This grandpa tree is a **clonal tree**, which means that it has regenerated new trunks, branches and roots over **thousands of years**, rather than being just one old tree. The oldest individual tree is a **5062-year-old Great Basin bristlecone pine** in the Rocky Mountains.

The oldest living tree is older than both **Stonehenge** and the **Great Pyramids** by hundreds of years! It's the oldest living organism on Earth.

Ring of fire

The rings of a tree are what tell us a tree's age, but that's not all they do! These rings can also tell us what the climate was like on Earth in the past, and even when volcanos have exploded. Hot stuff!

It's good to talk

Trees talk to one another. They share nutrients through an underground internet of soil fungi and can also warn each other of incoming insect attack by sending chemical signals through the air.

WE DRINK THE SAME WATER THAT THE DINOSAURS DRANK

Next time you are guzzling down a glass of cold refreshing water, pause for a second to think about the fact that dinosaurs were drinking that very same water about **65 million years ago**. The water on Earth today is the very same that's always been here – it's been recycled for over **4 billion years**! Water travels around Earth in a continuous movement, making a circuit from the oceans to the atmosphere to the Earth's surface, over and over again in an endless cycle. It's believed that no new water has been created since this cycle first began, and only the tiniest amount has evaporated into space. Our water has been with us a long time and will continue to be with us for longer still.

It came from outer space

Water on Earth arrived on asteroids and comets **4.5 billion years ago**.

Water of life

The average person drinks about **1000 litres** of water every year. You can survive without food for a whole month, but you'd only last a week without water.

Water, water everywhere

About **71%** of the Earth's surface is water. If you took all the water on Earth and put it into a ball, it would be about **1384 kilometres wide**.

A bit salty

Humans are only able to drink **1%** of all the water on Earth – **97%** of the world's water is salty or undrinkable, and the other **2%** is locked in glaciers and ice caps.

THERE'S A PLACE ON EARTH THAT'S CLOSER TO THE INTERNATIONAL SPACE STATION (ISS) THAN IT IS TO LAND

There's a point in the South Pacific Ocean that is the literal middle of nowhere. It's called **Point Nemo** and it's the spot in the ocean farthest away from land – **2688 kilometres away**, to be precise. It's not the kind of place you want to go to on your holidays though – there's no land there, just water and lots of it!

When the International Space Station (ISS) makes one of its **15 daily orbits** around the globe, it passes directly over Point Nemo at an average height of **400 kilometres**. What this means is that at those moments in time, the ISS is closer to Point Nemo than Point Nemo is to land!

Graveyard shift

Point Nemo's remote location makes it the ideal spot to get rid of space junk. Hundreds of decommissioned Soviet and Russian space vessels, as well as some Japanese and European crafts, have all been given a watery grave at Point Nemo. This is where the lonely spot gets the nickname the **'Spacecraft Cemetery'**.

Getting away from it all

Point Nemo is located at **48°52.6'S 123°23.6'W**. It's an incredibly isolated area of the South Pacific Ocean. To the north is **Ducie Island**, a tiny, uninhabited atoll. To the northeast is **Motu Nui,** the largest of three islets just south of Easter Island. And to the south is the snow-covered **Maher Island**, part of Antarctica. Between these three points there is nothing but ocean.

Size it up

Point Nemo is **22,405,411 square kilometres** of ocean, an area larger than the entire former Soviet Union, the largest country in modern history!

Blooper

Point Nemo is also home to **The Bloop**, a very loud, ultra-low-frequency noise, which is the sound of ice fracturing in Antarctica. The Bloop is one of the loudest underwater sounds ever recorded.

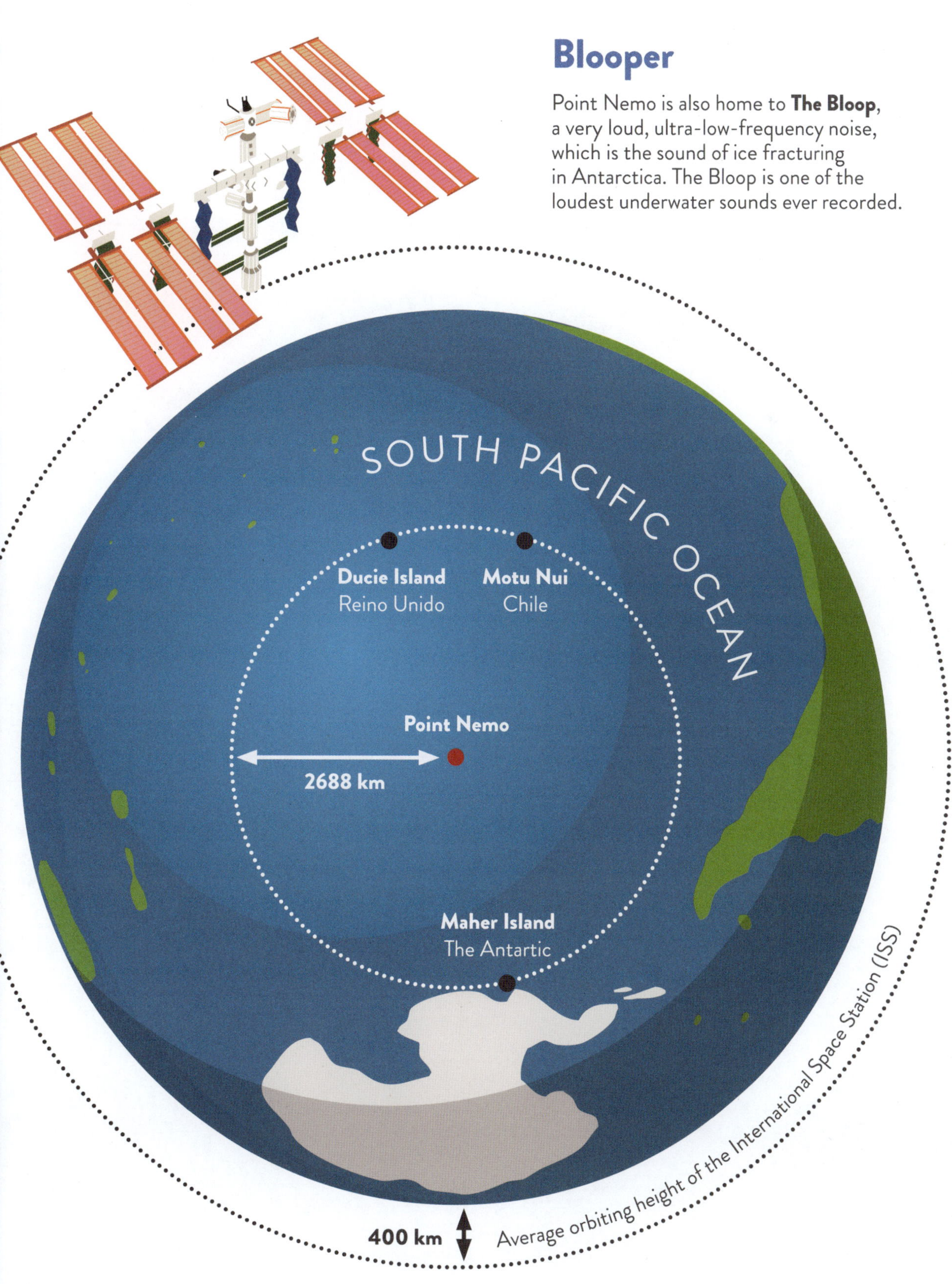

EARTH CHALLENGE

On the next blue-sky day with fluffy clouds, see if you can count each cloud and estimate the volume of water floating in the fluffy shapes above you.

FLUFFY CLOUDS WEIGH HALF A MILLION KILOGRAMS

Imagine lying on your back on a beautiful day and looking up at the bright blue sky filled with fluffy clouds. One minute, the clouds look like an ice cream, but moments later they appear to be a face or an animal.

Those little white clouds you see dotted around the sky may look light and fluffy, but they are actually extremely heavy! They're called **cumulus clouds** and on average they weigh an astonishing **500,000 kilograms**!

As well as cumulus clouds, there are also **cirrus clouds** (which are thin and wispy), **stratus clouds** (that form a huge, grey blanket across the sky) and **nimbus clouds** (the dark clouds you see during a thunderstorm).

Shape shifters

The wonderful ever-changing shapes of cumulus clouds are caused by the air that surrounds them. The clouds are affected by the air temperature, which is constantly changing. When it's windy, the clouds are pushed and pulled, which results in their fantastic variety of shapes.

The elephant in the room

To put the weight of a cumulus cloud into perspective, **500,000 kilograms** is equal to **100 elephants**!

Floating on air

Clouds are made up of water, and water is heavier than air. So how do clouds float? Although most clouds do contain a large amount of water, it's spread out across a giant area in the form of very, very small droplets or crystals. They are so small that gravity hardly affects them.

THE AMAZON RIVER HAS NO BRIDGES

The Amazon River in South America is the longest river in the world. It runs through Guyana, Ecuador, Venezuela, Bolivia, Brazil, Colombia and Peru, and spans over **6575 kilometres**! The Amazon is surrounded by an epic jungle, filled with breathtakingly beautiful waterfalls and home to the world's largest river dolphins. But one thing the Amazon doesn't have is any bridges – not a single one! If you want to cross from one side to the other, you'll need to grab a boat or jump on a ferry.

Rain check

During the rainy season, the river rises up to **10 metres** and some crossings can be as wide as **190 kilometres**. The riverbanks are constantly eroding too, making it a nightmare for any engineer to even think about planning a bridge.

Pleased to meat you

You don't want to take a cooling dip in the Amazon, as it's home to the **piranha** – a fish that eats meat! Piranhas are known to attack in groups, eating any unfortunate animal that strays into the water!

Road to nowhere

Another reason for the lack of bridges is that the Amazon doesn't need them. The majority of the river runs through dense rainforests which are hardly populated, except for a few large cities. And anyone travelling around the region uses the river itself as their main highway.

Snake eyes

Piranhas aren't the only meat eaters to avoid in the Amazon; this river is also home to the heaviest snake in the world, the green anaconda. They can grow up to almost **10 metres** in length, with a girth of around **90–115 centimetres** and can weigh **120 kilograms**.

BALLS OF LIGHTNING CAN BREAK INTO YOUR HOME

Of all the natural phenomena on Earth, **ball lightning**, small glowing orbs with electric tendrils, has to be one of the most mysterious. These strange balls of electricity often appear before or after thunderstorms, sometimes within a few seconds of lightning, but normally with no connection to the lightning bolt. The glowing sphere will move in the air at walking speed before disappearing roughly **10 seconds** after it first emerged. If this wasn't fantastic enough, there are accounts of the balls entering buildings through closed and open windows, or sometimes just materialising inside. Imagine *that* appearing in your living room!

Burning questions

There is so much mystery around indoor ball lightning. What causes it to appear? How and why does it move against the direction of the wind? Why doesn't it seem to damage the indoor environment it appears in? At the moment these questions remain unanswered, but one theory is that these weird orbs are not lightning, but actually light trapped inside a sphere of thin air.

Ups and downs

Perhaps even scarier than seeing ball lightning in your home is seeing it in a plane or on a submarine. Ball lightning has been sighted in many spooky places; it's even been observed travelling down the central aisle of a plane and right through a flight attendant!

Aglow

These floating luminescent balls can glow as brightly as a **100-watt lightbulb** and can sometimes be as big as a beachball!

The cities with the world's biggest populations are **Tokyo** (Japan), **Delhi** (India), **Shanghai** (China), **São Paulo** (Brazil) and **Mexico City** (Mexico). The city with the smallest population in the world is **Hum** (Croatia) where there are just **30 people**.

THERE ARE MORE PEOPLE LIVING INSIDE THIS CIRCLE THAN OUTSIDE OF IT

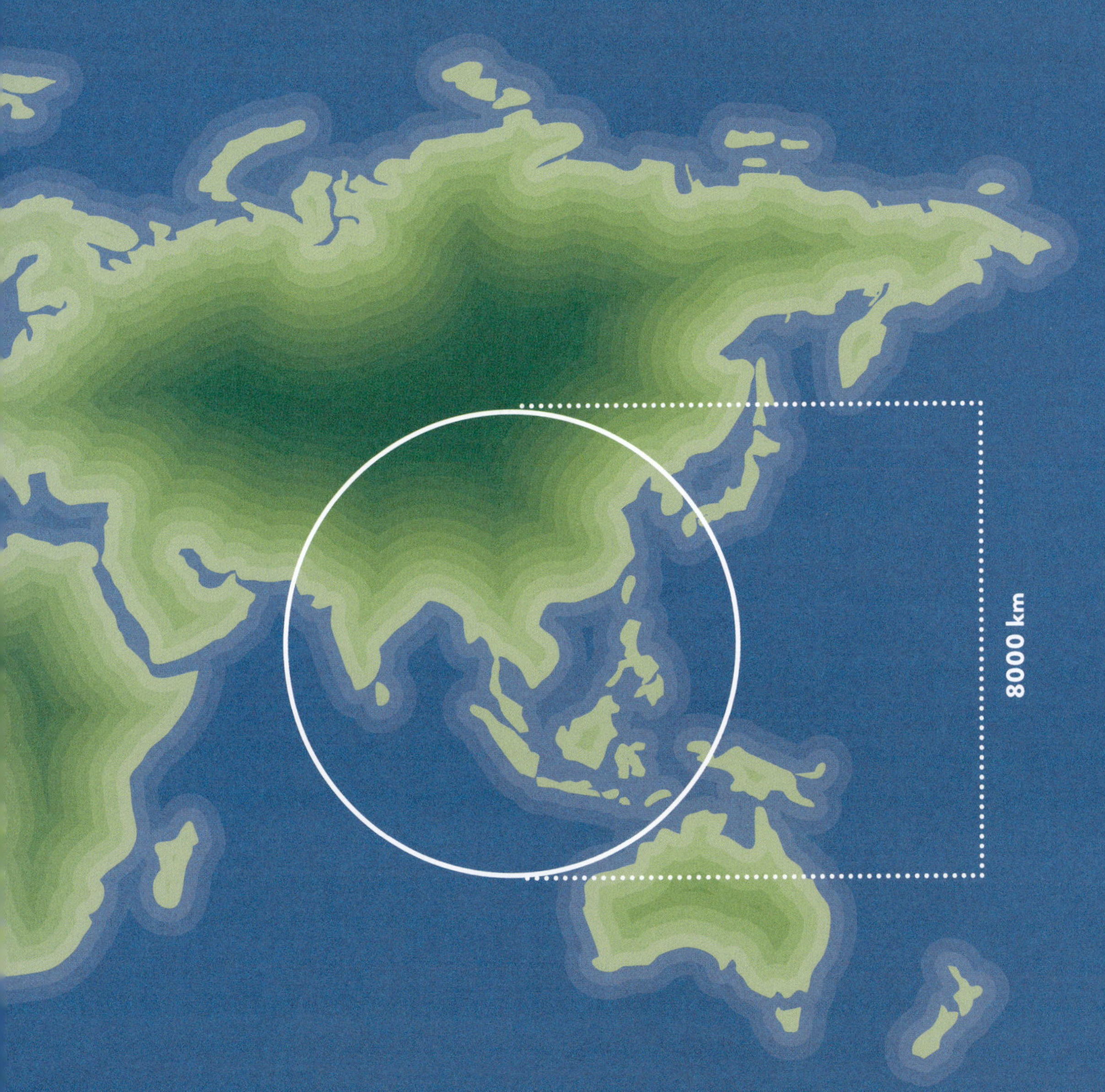

There may be **7.8 billion people** living on Earth, but we're not all evenly distributed around the planet. Less of us live in deserts than along coastlines, and there are now more people calling cities their home than ever before.

Over half of the human population live in just one area, which is only around **8000 kilometres** in diameter! The **21 countries** inside that circle include **China, India** and **Southeast Asian countries**. However, the circle only accounts for about **one sixth** of the Earth's total land. Just to make things even more interesting, the circle also happens to include one of the least populated countries in the world, **Mongolia**, which is mostly covered in water.

4.5 billion years ago

4 billion years ago

3 billion years ago

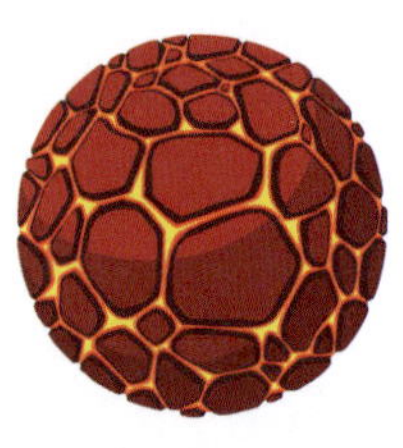

4.543 billion years ago
The Earth is formed.

4.51 billion years ago
The Moon is formed.

3.5 billion years ago
The oldest evidence of life emerges in the form of bacteria and single-celled organisms.

2.45 billion years ago
The start of Earth's oxygen-rich atmosphere.

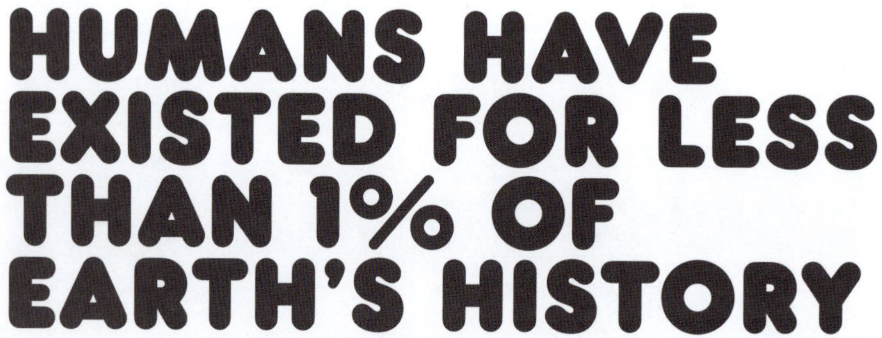

HUMANS HAVE EXISTED FOR LESS THAN 1% OF EARTH'S HISTORY

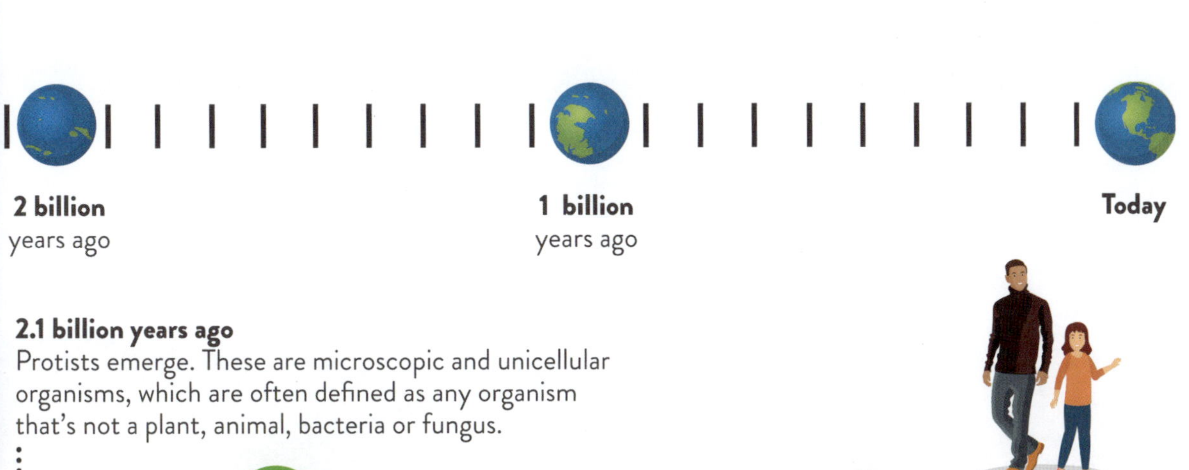

2.1 billion years ago
Protists emerge. These are microscopic and unicellular organisms, which are often defined as any organism that's not a plant, animal, bacteria or fungus.

Today
Humans walk the Earth.

240 million years ago
Dinosaurs roam the Earth.

520 million years ago
Hard-shelled animals appear in oceans.

1 billion years ago
Plants and fungi emerge.

Spread both your arms straight out from your shoulders and imagine that the entire history of Earth is represented by the distance between the fingertips of each of your hands. Pretend that everything that has ever happened on Earth, including its formation, fits in the spaces from the fingertips of your left hand all the way across to your right. This timeline includes the origin of the first primitive single-celled lifeforms to the lives of the dinosaurs, and eventually the birth of humanity! All of this has happened over **4.543 billion years**. If you took a nail file out and shortened the fingernail of your longest finger, you'd be wiping out all of human history!

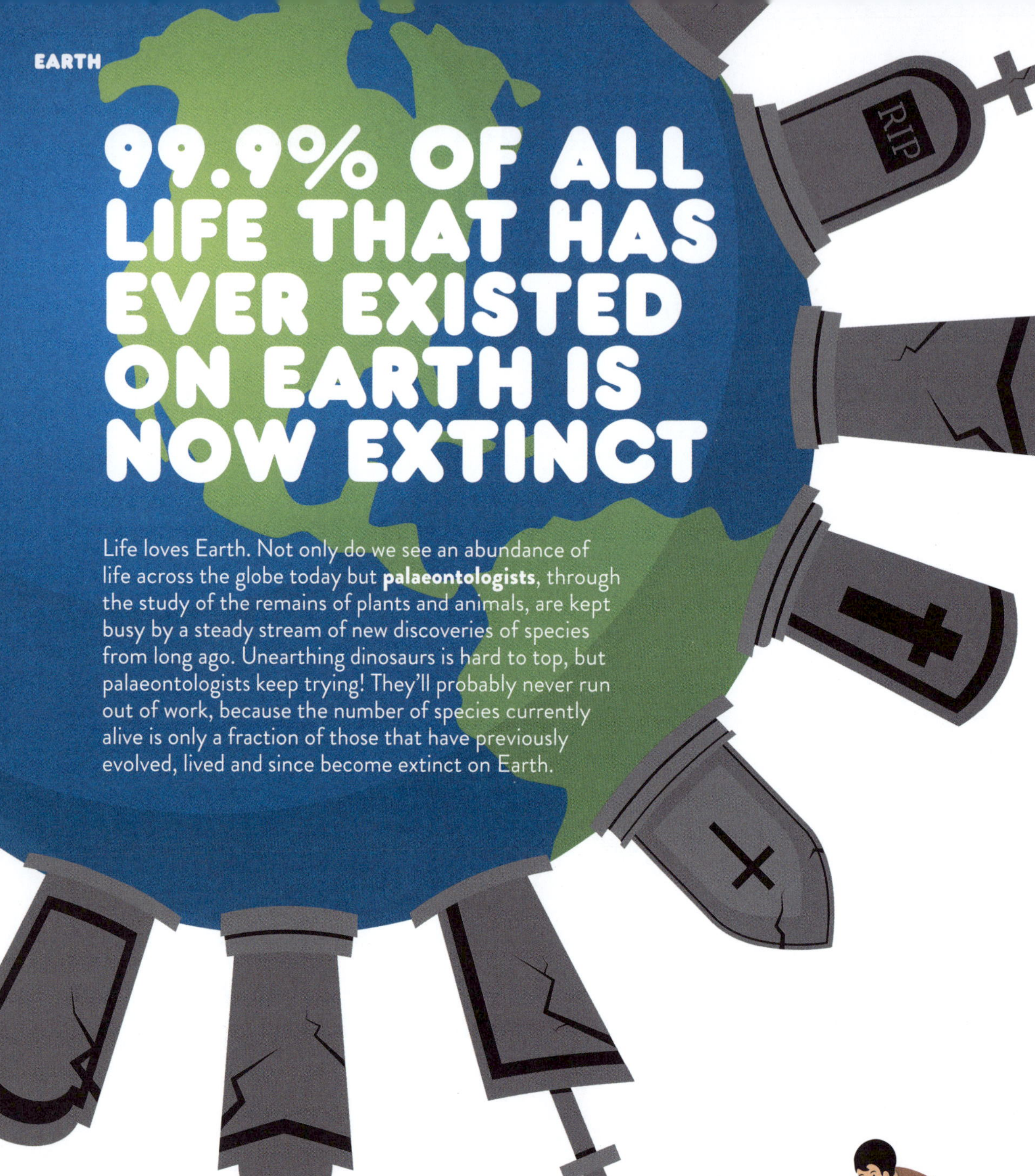

99.9% OF ALL LIFE THAT HAS EVER EXISTED ON EARTH IS NOW EXTINCT

Life loves Earth. Not only do we see an abundance of life across the globe today but **palaeontologists**, through the study of the remains of plants and animals, are kept busy by a steady stream of new discoveries of species from long ago. Unearthing dinosaurs is hard to top, but palaeontologists keep trying! They'll probably never run out of work, because the number of species currently alive is only a fraction of those that have previously evolved, lived and since become extinct on Earth.

Dig in

Palaeontologists can tell that most species tend to hang around for anything between **1 million** to **11 million years**. Modern humans have been around for **200,000 years** so far.

Done to death

Rather worryingly, there have been five mass extinctions in the history of Earth. It seems as if old age isn't the only reason why a species dies out.

The first was **444 million years ago**, when **85%** of all species on Earth died as the planet froze over.

The second was **375 million years ago**. **75%** of all life suffocated as oxygen was sucked from the water; scientists suspect this may have been the result of algal blooms.

The biggest extinction of all was the third, around **250 million years ago**. A mind-blowing **96%** of all life on Earth was extinguished as temperatures surged, and the oceans acidified and stagnated.

The mysterious fourth extinction was **200 million years ago**. No clear cause has yet been discovered for the extinction of around **80%** of life at this time.

The mass extinction that annihilated the dinosaurs was the most recent, devastating the Earth only **65 million years ago**. Scientists are pretty certain that this extinction was caused by a large meteorite hitting the Earth and killing off **76%** of life.

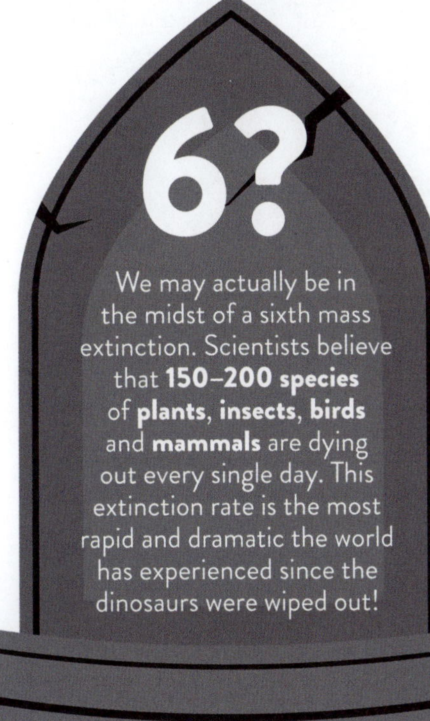

We may actually be in the midst of a sixth mass extinction. Scientists believe that **150–200 species** of **plants, insects, birds** and **mammals** are dying out every single day. This extinction rate is the most rapid and dramatic the world has experienced since the dinosaurs were wiped out!

Disappearing act

Human activity is now directly influencing extinction. We've witnessed the disappearance of **60%** of animal life since 1970. The world's environmental experts are warning that the annihilation of wildlife is an emergency that threatens the future of our planet.

IF THE EARTH WAS AN APPLE, THEN WE HAVEN'T EVEN SUNK OUR TEETH THROUGH THE SKIN YET

Humans haven't drilled very far at all into Earth's surface. If we shrunk the Earth down to the size of an apple, then the crust would be as thin as the skin. Not only have we not taken a sizeable bite out of our apple-sized Earth yet, but we haven't even managed to get through the skin!

Hole in one

If there was a hole right through the Earth, it would take **42 minutes** to fall from one side to the other. You would also clock up a speed of **28,440 kilometres an hour**, ignoring air resistance and the extreme heat, of course. Wow!

42 minutes is almost as long as half a football match or an episode of TV! It's long enough that the fall through the Earth may even get a little boring.

Shell shocked

It may seem like the Earth is made up of one big solid rock, but it's really made of a number of spherical shells, some of which are constantly moving!

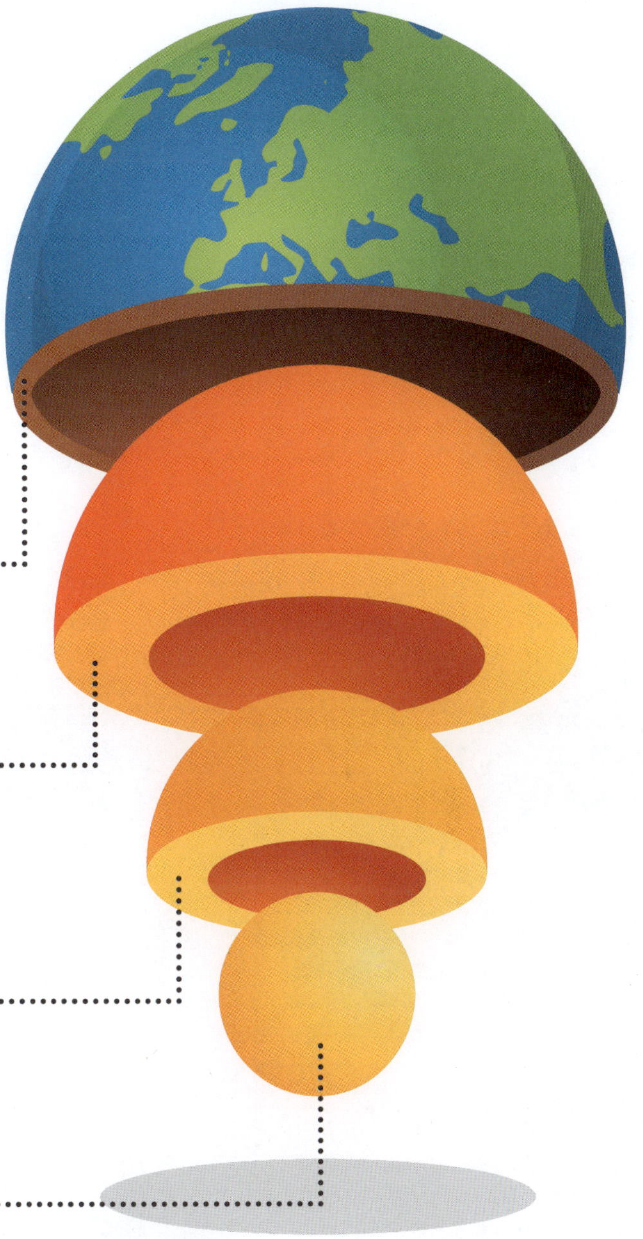

Crust

The Earth's surface is covered by its thinnest layer, the crust. The crust accounts for less than **1%** of the Earth's volume. This layer of the Earth varies from around **5 kilometres** on the ocean floor to **70 kilometres** thick on land inhabited by humans called the **continental crust**.

Mantle

This makes up about **84%** of the Earth's volume. The mantle is predominantly solid, but it behaves like a viscous fluid and is about **2900 kilometres** thick.

Outer core

This is the only liquid layer of the Earth and is **2300 kilometres** thick. The outer core makes up about **15%** of the planet's volume, and is responsible for Earth's protective magnetic field.

Inner core

The Earth's inner core is between **1230 kilometres** and **1530 kilometres** thick, and accounts for less than **1%** of Earth's volume!

Dig deep

A group from the Soviet Union once started digging to see how deep a hole they could make. After almost two decades of constant work, they'd only managed to go down **12 kilometres** – that's about **0.1%** of the way through the planet.

THE MARIANA TRENCH IS DEEPER THAN MOUNT EVEREST IS HIGH

Angler fish
2000 metres

The deepest natural point on Earth's surface is at the bottom of the **Mariana Trench**. Located in the western Pacific Ocean, the maximum known depth is **11,034 metres**.

If you were to drop Mount Everest into the trench, it would comfortably fit below the surface with a little more than **2 kilometres** of water above it. So far, only **8 people** have been to the bottom of the Mariana Trench – whereas there have been more than **4000** who have reached the top of Mt Everest! Among those who have reached the bottom of Mariana's Trench are the oceanographers Don Walsh and Jacques Piccard, who descended in a submersible in 1960.

In 2012, Canadian film director James Cameron travelled to the bottom of the trench, and, more recently, former astronaut Kathy Sullivan did the same.

What was remarkable about Kathy Sullivan's descent was that **25 years earlier** she had become the first woman from the United States to **walk in space**. What a legend!

In the dark

Light can travel as far as **1000 metres** down in the ocean, but beyond a depth of **200 metres** the light becomes far weaker, dimming as you go deeper until it's barely noticeable at all.

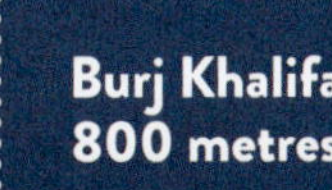

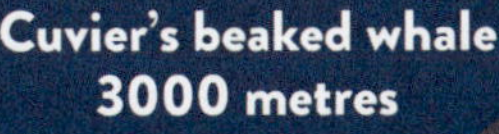

Dumped on

A plastic bag has been found at the bottom of the trench. This is the deepest piece of garbage we've ever found, with scientists making the discovery at **10,898 metres**. The plastic bag was one of over **3000** pieces of man-made waste found in the trench that dated back **30 years**.

EARTH WAS ONCE A FROZEN SNOWBALL

We've all felt that kind of cold weather that makes us wrap up in our warm clothes, woollen hats, scarves, and maybe even gloves. Now imagine if the coldest weather you'd ever experienced got even colder, and then stuck around for **120 million years**! That's exactly what happened on Earth **750 million years ago**! Our planet went from a tropical paradise covered in warm waters that teemed with life to an almost lifeless snowball with howling winds whistling across a cold, barren and ice-covered landscape. Frosty!

Wild and woolly

The most recent ice age, just a short **2.6 million years ago**, led to the rise of the woolly mammoth and the vast expansion of glaciers on Earth.

Cold as ice

In Earth's **4.5-billion-year** history, scientists believe there have been at least **five major ice ages**.

The **Huronian ice age** was one of the longest ice ages in the Earth's history and spanned between **2.4** to **2.1 billion years ago**.

The **Cryogenian ice age** occurred from **850** to **635 million years ago**. This ice age was so cold that ice sheets reached all the way to the equator!

The **Andean-Saharan ice age**: between **460** to **430 million years ago**.

The **Karoo ice age** lasted around **100 million years**, between **360** to **260 million years ago**.

The **Quaternary ice age** is the most recent. It began **2.5 million years ago** and is still going now! We are currently in an **interglacial stage** of this ice age.

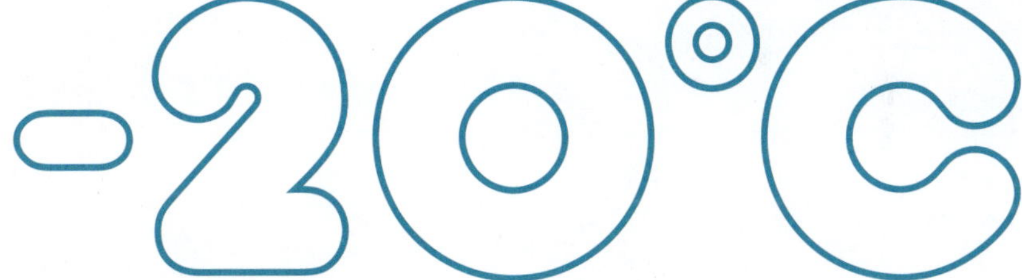

This was the average temperature **715 million years ago** at the equator, which is traditionally the warmest place on Earth. This is the same temperature as Antarctica today!

Being in our **interglacial period** means that Earth is enjoying warmer global temperatures, which can last for thousands of years before we go back to glacial periods (times where large sheets of ice cover the Earth).

THE LARGEST ORGANISM ON EARTH IS A FUNGUS

Most tourists wandering through **Malheur National Forest** in the US state of Oregon are blissfully unaware that beneath their feet is one of the world's living wonders – and it's a fungus; a *parasitic* fungus. ***Armillaria ostoyae*** covers an area of more than **9.6 square kilometres**, and invades other organisms to take their nutrients. Plus, it's still growing, making it the world's largest known living thing!

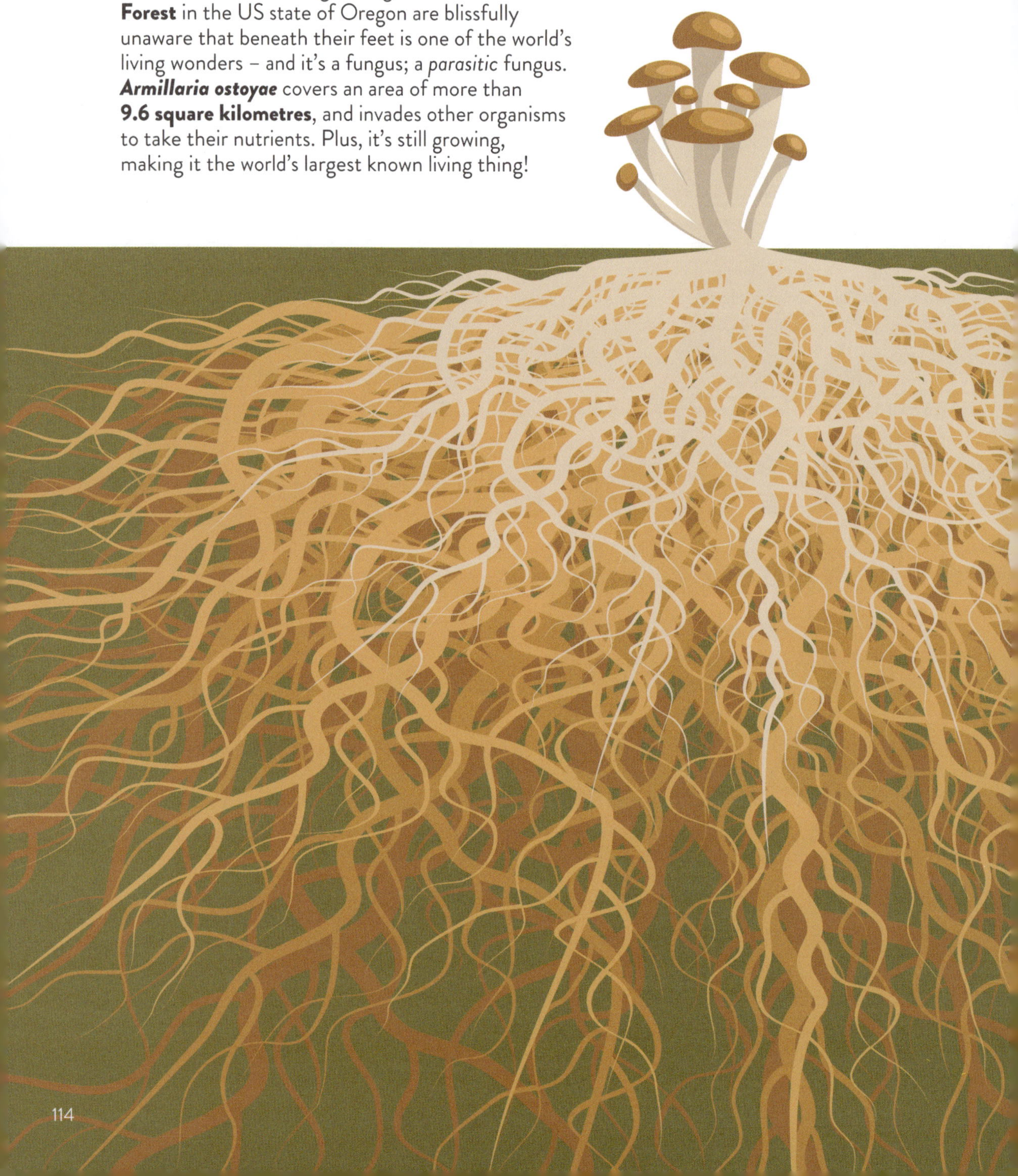

Going underground

Armillaria ostoyae generates honey mushrooms, which grow above ground. These mushrooms are only the surface blooms of a much larger underground mat of threads that draw nutrients from nearby vegetation.

Eat and run

As the parasitic fungus grew over the course of thousands of years, any tree or shrub in its path was infected, killed, eaten and then engulfed. This process is important to the forest ecosystem, as it allows different species to move into the gaps the fungus leaves behind. It encourages nutrient recycling too, so if a tree dies it goes back into the soil and provides nutrients for the trees that grow in its place.

THE FUNGUS IS 2400 YEARS OLD

To get an idea of just how big this giant **9.6 square kilometre** fungus actually is, picture a football field. Pretty big, right? Now try to imagine **1344 fields** all stuck together. Woah, that's one big fungus!

THERE IS A THAT DOE

You might think that it's impossible to have a country with only **50 people**, but the residents of **Sealand** would disagree with you. This **micronation** is an offshore WWII anti-aircraft platform, and it's located just **13 kilometres** off the coast of Suffolk, England.

In **1967**, Roy Bates and his family took over the platform, cheekily taking advantage of its uncertain status as it lay outside of British-controlled waters. Bates immediately declared the platform an independent principality and set up a micronation along with a Sealand government. And this was how the world's smallest country was born! However, Sealand holds no official recognition from other counties, as they refuse to acknowledge its existence.

COUNTRY N'T EXIST

Everything under the sun

Sealand has everything that any other country has: a constitution, flag, currency, stamps, a national anthem and passports. It even has its own football team!

Your highness

Roy Bates claimed the title of the **Prince of Sealand**, and although he and his family moved back to the mainland England they continued to rule the platform like royalty. Like all royal families, the rulers of Sealand have passed their royal titles from parents to children. Roy's son Michael is now the Prince of Sealand.

Space invaders

In 1978, Prince Roy had to defend his country from invaders when a team of armed men stormed the platform and kidnapped his son! Roy managed to reclaim his country and free his son by kidnapping the lawyer of the man behind the attack.

THE EARTH MAY BE JUST AS ALIVE AS YOU ARE

Imagine that the Earth and all the life on it were not actually separate from one another, but behaved as one being, all the living and non-living elements working in perfect harmony together. Imagine that humans and all other living creatures were not just inhabitants of the Earth, but were the Earth!

This hypothetical super-being is called the ***Gaia Hypothesis***. Although it may sound far-fetched, the idea of a living planet which is as alive as the birds, the bees and all the humans around you, is absolutely fascinating.

EARTH CHALLENGE

Plant some seeds at home. Watch how, by watering the soil regularly and supplying it with the right amount of sunlight, they germinate to grow strong and tall.

Stranger things

Gaia Hypothesis could help explain some of the stranger features of the Earth. For example, why the oceans aren't a lot saltier, or why the atmosphere is not largely carbon dioxide.

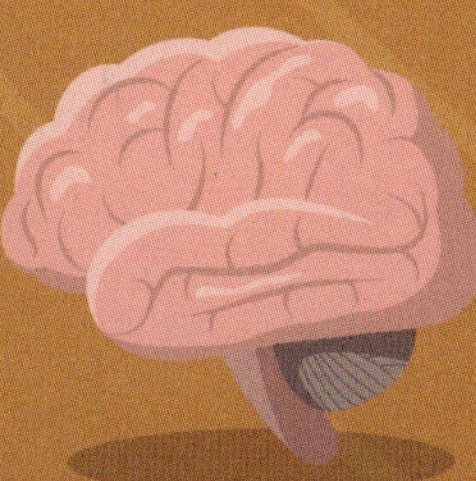

Brain box

If the *Gaia Hypothesis* is true, then humans may very well be the brain or the consciousness of Earth. We could be the Earth becoming aware it's alive!

Larger than life

If the *Gaia Hypothesis* is to be believed, then all of the plants, animals and insects on the planet would have actually evolved to regulate the chemistry of the biosphere. The air, water and soil are the major components of one giant central organism.

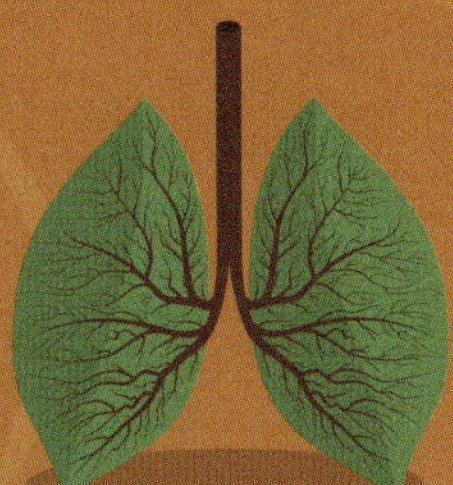

Breathe it in

The Earth is breathing, sweating and changing! There are literally millions of organisms that tirelessly consume and replenish the air, water and rock on this planet. All at once, everything on Earth is growing and changing together.

SEEING EARTH FROM SPACE CHANGES YOU FOREVER

Of the hundreds of people who have travelled into space for the first time and seen the Earth in its entirety, many described the feeling of looking down on their home planet as an overwhelming and almost mystical shift in perception. This experience is known as the **'overview effect'**. These space travellers were able to see that Earth is a single planet with a life-supporting atmosphere, shared by everyone who lives here – our collective home in the universe.

In 1968, an image of Earth drifting in the darkness of space with the moon's surface in the foreground, was captured for the very first time. The iconic shot was snapped from onboard **Apollo 8**, and became known as **'Earthrise'**. It's often described as the most influential environmental photograph ever taken.

Handle with care

Once astronauts look down at the Earth from space and see this amazing, beautiful planet from a new perspective, they often describe it as a living and breathing organism. The astronauts also say that the Earth looks extremely fragile, with a visible paper-thin layer of atmosphere as the only thing that is protecting us from the cold vacuum of space.

Cosmic ray

Astronauts are blessed with a cosmic perspective; they are able to see the Earth as a planet and the Sun as a blinding white star. Down here on Earth we see the yellow Sun in a blue sky, but up there the white light of the Sun is clear against the blackness of space.

299792
km/s

NCE
Greatest Human Ever
Norman Borlaug

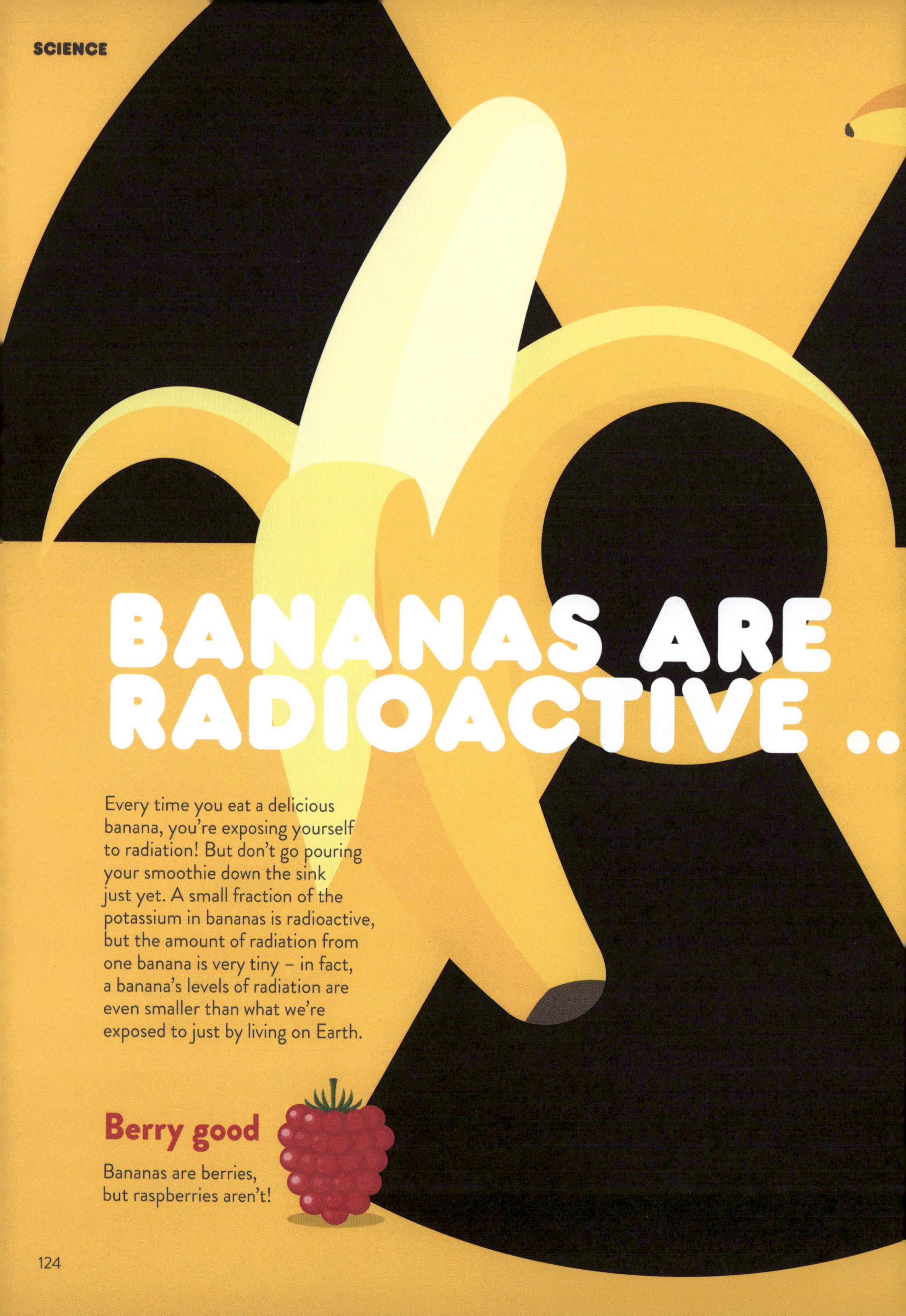

BANANAS ARE RADIOACTIVE ..

Every time you eat a delicious banana, you're exposing yourself to radiation! But don't go pouring your smoothie down the sink just yet. A small fraction of the potassium in bananas is radioactive, but the amount of radiation from one banana is very tiny – in fact, a banana's levels of radiation are even smaller than what we're exposed to just by living on Earth.

Berry good

Bananas are berries, but raspberries aren't!

Going bananas

To measure the amount of damage radiation would do to a human body, scientists use a unit called **sieverts**. Eating a banana is the equivalent to **0.1 sieverts**, to put that in context:

0.1 sieverts

An airport security scan is **0.25 sieverts**, the same amount of radiation as eating **two and a half bananas**.

... AND CAN WALK

Not only are bananas radioactive, but the trees they grow on can walk! These trees can move up to **40 centimetres**, but don't worry, this is more down to how they grow them than anything that occurs naturally.

Bananas are cultivated by using two shoots. One of the shoots is used immediately, while the other is left to grow so it's ready to produce bananas in about **7 months**. As the shoots grow, they move along the ground, meaning that over a long period of time the whole plant will have shifted from its original position all of its own accord!

A dental X-ray is **5 sieverts**, which is the same as eating **50 bananas**.

A fatal dose of radiation is **10 million sieverts**, which means you'd have to eat **100 million bananas** for the radiation to kill you – but you'd probably die from a tummy ache first!

EVERY SECOND, 65 BILLION NEUTRINOS PASS THROUGH YOUR FINGERNAIL

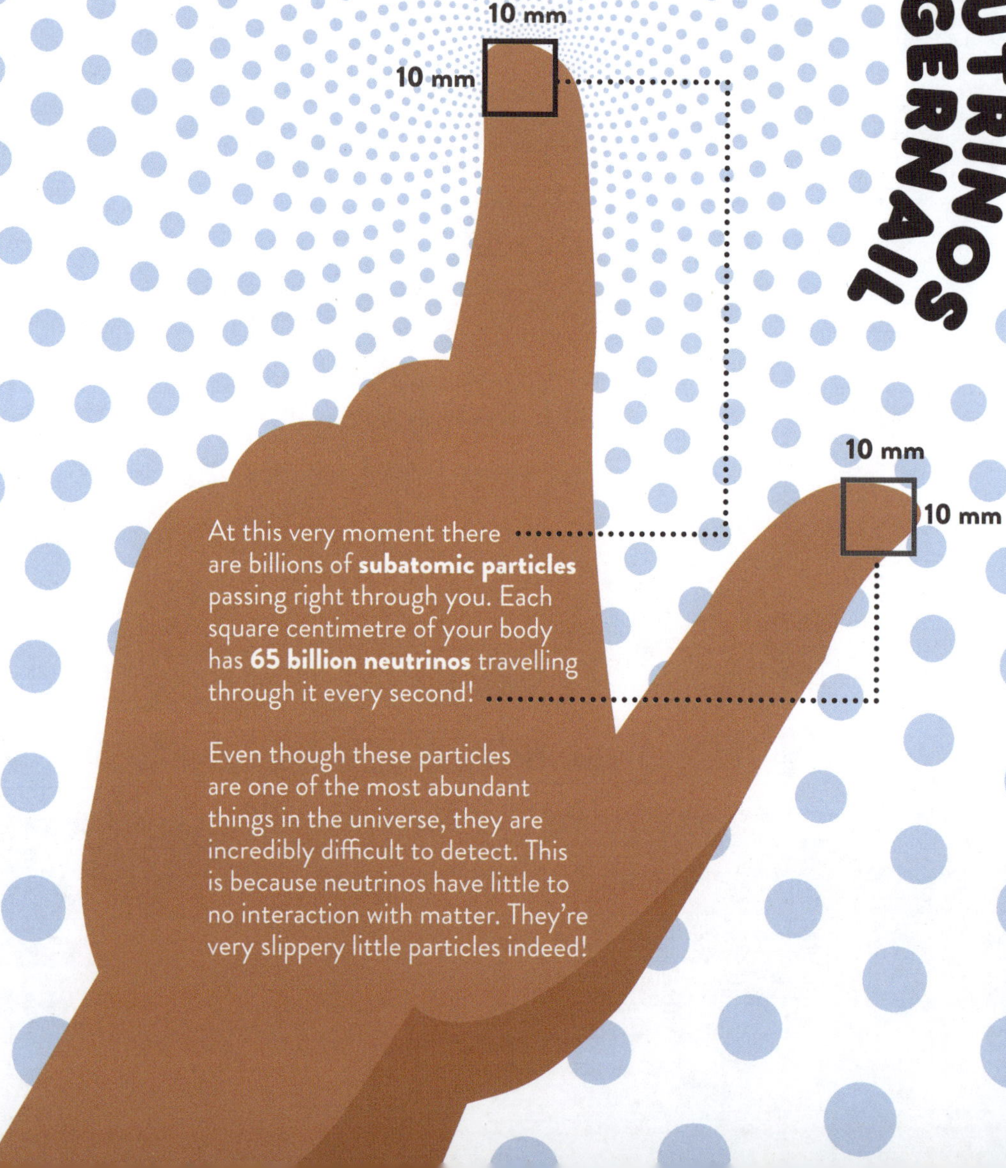

10 mm

10 mm

10 mm

10 mm

At this very moment there are billions of **subatomic particles** passing right through you. Each square centimetre of your body has **65 billion neutrinos** travelling through it every second!

Even though these particles are one of the most abundant things in the universe, they are incredibly difficult to detect. This is because neutrinos have little to no interaction with matter. They're very slippery little particles indeed!

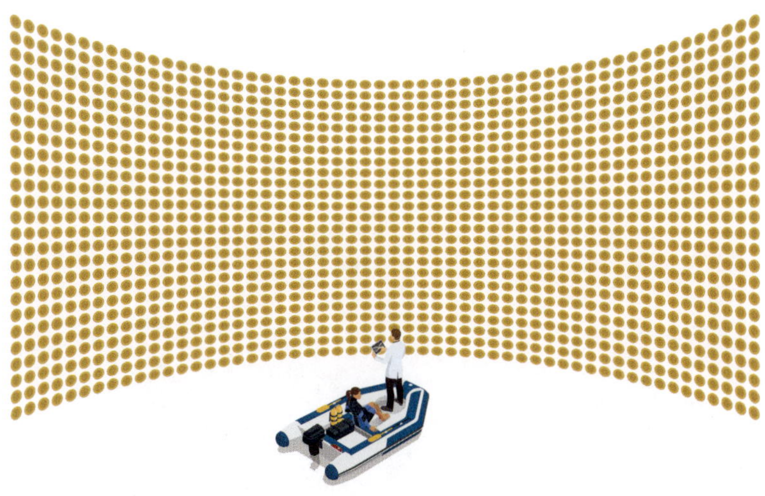

Pinpoint accuracy

Neutrinos may be difficult to detect, but not impossible. **1000** metres under **Mount Ikeno** in Japan is the **Super-Kamiokande detector**, which contains **50,000 litres** of super-pure water along with **13,000 sensors** to pinpoint any signs of neutrinos.

Speed demons

Neutrinos have almost no mass, but this doesn't slow them down. Neutrinos are fast, very fast. They travel across space and through entire planets at almost the speed of light!

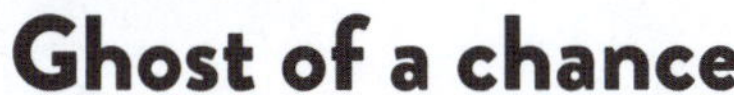

Ghost of a chance

Neutrinos are often nicknamed **'ghost particles'**. This is because of their almost non-existent mass and lack of interaction with other forces.

Force of nature

Many processes in nature create neutrinos: the Sun's nuclear reactions; particle decays in the Earth; when stars go super-nova and explodes. Humans have also produced neutrinos inside particle accelerators and nuclear power plants!

HOT WATER FREEZES FASTER THAN COLD WATER

You'd think that, by now, humans would have mastered the art of something as simple as freezing water. But it turns out we still have more to learn! It's perfectly reasonable to assume that hot water takes longer to cool down than cold water, and it would therefore take longer to freeze. But actually, the opposite is true, and under certain conditions hot water can freeze faster than cold water!

Cream of the crop

The strange phenomenon of the fast-freezing hot water is known as the **Mpemba effect**, named after Erasto Mpemba. Erasto was making ice cream as part of a school project in 1963 when he noticed that his scorching hot mixture of boiled cream and sugar froze significantly quicker than the mixture of his classmates who had let theirs cool.

Take five

Although the reason why hot water freezes faster than cold remains a mystery, there are some theories as to why this takes place:

A hot beaker will melt the frost off its sides, losing any insulation, whereas the ice that forms around the beaker of cold water could actually help to retain heat and slow down the freezing process.

Cold water has more dissolved gases than hot water, which could play a role in the rate of cooling.

Water can sometimes supercool before freezing when the water freezes not at 0°C, but at some lower temperature. Hot water may experience less supercooling than cold water and therefore freeze faster.

Hot water loses more water molecules through evaporation, which means there is less of it to freeze.

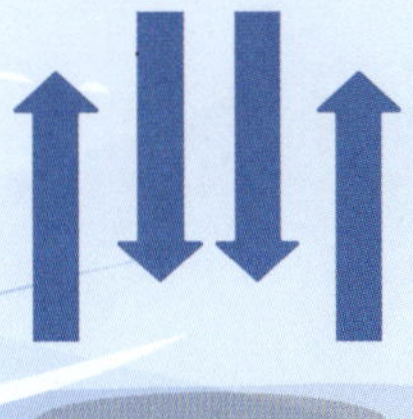

Hot water may freeze faster due to increased convection currents. Water mainly cools from its surface and the sides, which causes cold water to sink and warm water to rise up in its place. There are more of these currents in hot water, which could affect the rate of cooling.

Some people insist the Mpemba effect is a myth, partly because it is very hard to replicate the conditions required for it to take place. But one thing is for certain, even after all this time water is still surprising us!

Have you ever boiled water at high altitude? Perhaps when in the mountains. Did you notice it boiled a lot quicker? This is because the air pressure is lower at a higher altitude!

Triple whammy

Did you know that water can be a solid, liquid and gas all at the same time? This is known as the **'triple point'** and occurs where the solid, liquid, and gas transition curves meet, and the temperature and pressure are just right. The triple point for water is at just above freezing (**0.01°C**) and at a pressure of **0.006 atmosphere**.

TWO PARTICLES ON OPPOSITE SIDES OF THE UNIVERSE CAN AFFECT EACH OTHER INSTANTLY

Quantum mechanics is a body of scientific laws that describes the incredibly strange behaviour of atoms, photons, electrons and the other particles that make up our universe. It is essentially the brain-melting branch of physics that's concerned with things that are very small – so small that they require special microscopes and cameras to be observed!

Quantum entanglement is a phenomenon studied in quantum mechanics. When a laser beam is fired through a crystal, it causes an individual photon to be split into a pair of **entangled photons**. Amazingly, these two particles somehow remain linked to one another, so any action performed on one – like measuring it – will affect the other. This reaction still happens no matter how far apart the particles are, even when they're light years across the universe!

Caught speeding

The affected change in quantum entanglement seems to take place faster than the speed of light – it may even be immediate! The speed of light is, as we know, the speed limit of the universe. The speed of change for entangled particles should not be possible, which only adds to the mystery of this phenomenon!

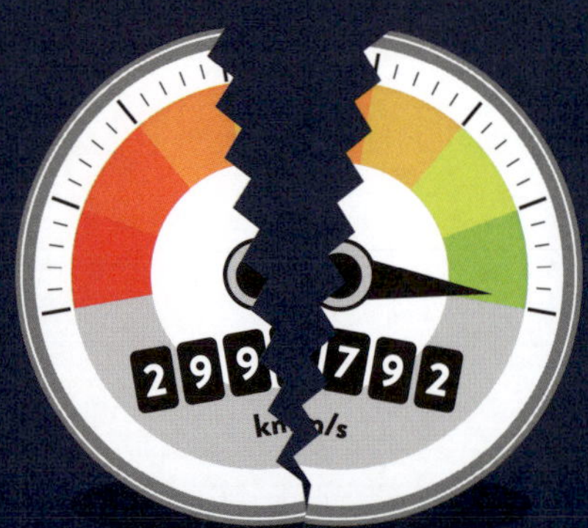

Don't worry if you find the idea of quantum mechanics extremely hard to understand. That's because it is! Scientists struggle with it too. As the famous physicist Richard Feynman once said: 'If you think you understand quantum mechanics, you don't understand quantum mechanics.'

Fog over

Unlike classic mechanics – which describes how things move at more standard speeds and sizes (like how a tennis ball travels through the air) – in quantum mechanics, objects exist in a fog of possibilities. There's a probability of being in one place and another chance of being at another.

Very spooky

Albert Einstein did not like the strangeness of quantum entanglement and referred to it as 'spooky action at a distance'.

THE ATOMIC BOMB WAS BUILT AND DETONATED 20 YEARS BEFORE WE HAD COLOUR TELEVISION

Atoms are so tiny that they're impossible to see with the naked eye. But when one is split into parts it sets off an explosive chain reaction that creates a blast so deadly and immense that it eviscerates everything around you in less than a second. The process of splitting an atom is how humans invented the atomic bomb, a terrifying creation that was a common household name before we even had colour television.

Time to split

Ernest Rutherford made history in 1917 when he split the atom in a nuclear reaction now known as **fission**. The **Allied Forces** of the Second World War were **Great Britain**, **France**, **the Soviet Union**, **the United States** and **China**. The Allies had begun discussing how nuclear fission might be used for military purposes to help them win the war. These conversations between the Allies in 1939 were where plans for the creation of an atomic bomb were made.

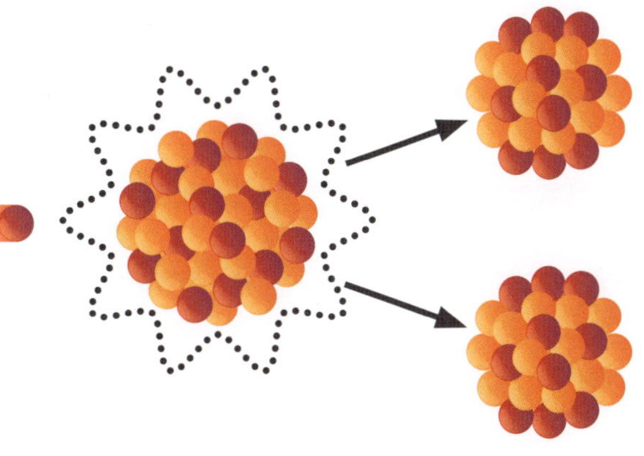

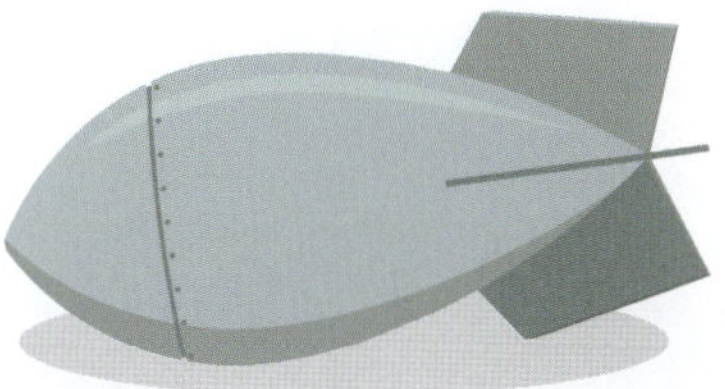

Bombshell

After plans for the atomic bomb were set in motion, Albert Einstein wrote to US President Franklin Roosevelt to give scientific support to the theory behind the atomic bomb. He also expressed concern that the Nazis were working on a powerful new weapon of their own. As a result, a nuclear weapon research and development group named the **Manhattan Project** was set up. In 1943, theory and practice came together when construction of the atomic bomb was completed.

Light up

In 1945 the atomic bomb was detonated in the Jornada del Muerto desert in New Mexico. An enormous mushroom cloud of searing light exploded **12 kilometres** into the air, powered by **18 million kilograms** of TNT. The explosion momentarily illuminated the surrounding mountains.

True colours

While these incredible leaps in military science were being made, TV lagged behind. Amazingly, it wasn't until **20 years later** that colour television sets started selling widely. The first all-colour TV series came in 1966, when viewers tuned in to the short-lived American sitcom called *The Marriage*. The era of black and white TV was over.

TIME ST THE SPEE

Although we cannot travel at the speed of light, Albert Einstein used to think about what would happen if we could. According to Einstein's Theory of Special Relativity, the faster you go, the slower time passes for you relative to your surroundings. This theory means that if you travelled at the speed of light, time would appear to stop. No way!

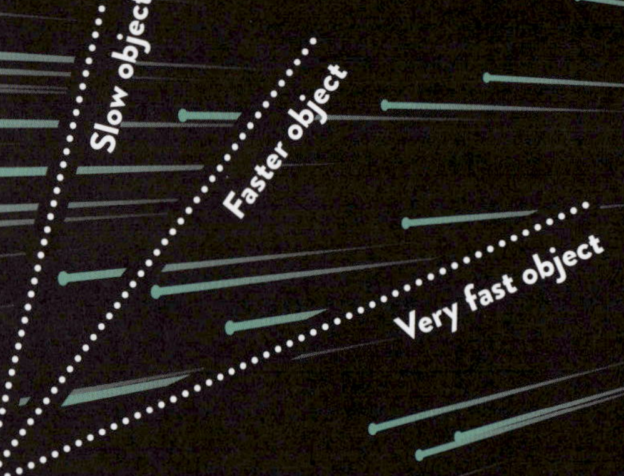

As the graph above shows, slower objects have faster passages of time than very fast objects, for which time passes much more slowly. When an object reaches the speed of light, it will hit zero on the time axis, which means that it will not have moved at all in the time direction. In other words, when the speed of light is reached, time stops for the traveller!

To infinity and beyond

As things approach the speed of light, they become heavier. If you were travelling at the speed limit of the universe, your mass would climb so high that it would start to reach infinity! It would require endless energy to move at that weight, which is why it's only possible for us to reach the speed of light in our imaginations.

Photons, the particles that make up light, have a mass of zero. The non-existent weight of light is why it's able to move at such incredible speed!

ALL OBJECTS FALL AT THE SAME SPEED

If you dropped a bowling ball and a feather from the top of a tall building, which do you think would hit the ground first? It's pretty safe to assume that it would be the bowling ball, as you'd think the feather would gently waft down to the ground while the bowling ball would plummet down. And that is exactly what would happen. But even though the objects would hit the ground at different times, in fact, all objects actually fall at the same speed, no matter what their mass is. The different falling speeds we witness as the objects drop is all to do with **air resistance**.

Floating on air

A falling feather is so light that the air offers much greater resistance to it than it does to the bowling ball. The air is an upward force of friction, which counteracts gravity and slows down the speed at which the feather falls.

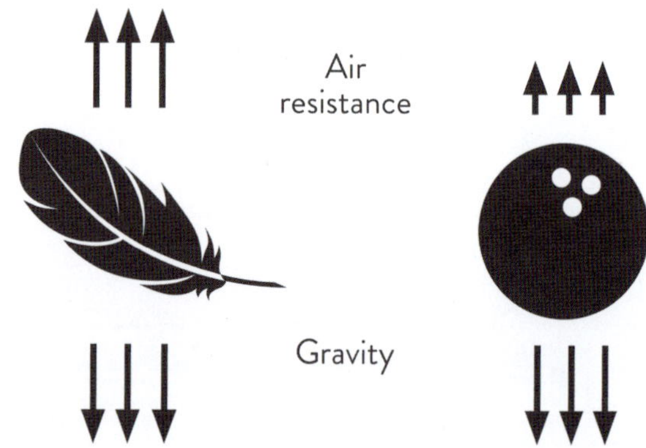

Under pressure

One way of experiencing air resistance yourself is to put your open hand out of the window of a moving car. Ask your parents' permission first though, and make sure to check there are no other cars around! When your hand is out, you'll be able to feel the air pressing against your hand. If the car speeds up, the air resistance force will get stronger. If you clench your hand into a tight fist, you'll feel that the force decreases due to less friction.

SCIENCE CHALLENGE

Take an apple and a feather, and drop them simultaneously from a good height to study their descent. Always check your surroundings before doing the experiment, and don't drop them on any people!

Vacuum up

We know that air resistance is the reason for the feather falling slowly because scientists have conducted the bowling ball and feather experiment by dropping the bowling ball and feather in more than one place. This includes a glass chamber that has had the air pumped out. This airless chamber creates a vacuum, and inside it the feather and bowling ball hit the ground at exactly the same after falling at exactly the same speed.

Mooning around

This amazing fact was even tested on the moon. In 1971, **Apollo 15 Commander David Scott** dropped a hammer and a feather (which was **44 times lighter** than the hammer!) and they both hit the ground simultaneously!

BICYCLES CAN

Bicycles are pretty amazing and zooming around on two wheels will definitely bring a huge smile to your face! But did you know that your bicycle can actually ride itself? If you give your riderless bicycle a good push (and it's travelling at just the right speed), it will balance itself and steer automatically to correct any wobbles it encounters. What makes this even more fascinating is that scientists still don't understand why a bicycle is as stable as it is, with or without a rider!

SCIENCE CHALLENGE

If you have a fidget spinner, give it a whirl and watch the gyroscopic effect in action. If you can't find a spinner, pay close attention to the casters on all the shopping trolleys next time you're in the supermarket and observe how they control the position of the wheel. Try using several different trolleys and observe the difference in motion on those with locked or broken wheels.

DE THEMSELVES

Fidgeting around

One idea as to why a bicycle can keep itself upright is the **gyroscopic theory**. This is where a bicycle is kept upright and stable by a spinning wheel. This is the same principle behind a fidget spinner, which is basically a pocket gyroscope.

Cast away

The **caster theory** says that a bicycle wheel is like a caster on a shopping trolley, where they automatically position themselves in the direction they are travelling. This is another potential reason why bicycles can keep themselves upright.

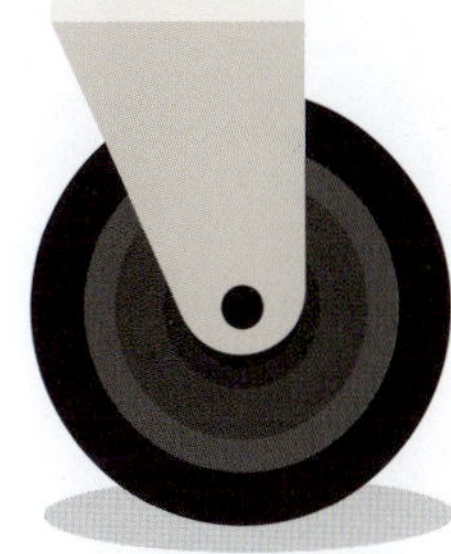

Balancing act

While the gyroscopic effect helps to explain the stability of a riderless bicycle and the caster effect makes it easier to ride, neither are responsible for a riderless bicycle's self-balancing effect, which is why the humble bicycle remains such a fascinating riding riddle.

LIFE DIDN'T GIVE US LEMONS, WE MADE THEM

When somebody talks about natural foods, the first things we think about are normally fruits and vegetables. These come to us straight from the Earth and are a delicious source of nutrition and vitamins. However, some fruits and vegetables are not quite as natural as you first think. In fact, some are actually man-made hybrids of selective breeding. Did you know that the original lemon was a hybrid between a male citron and a female sour orange, which itself was a hybrid of a pomelo and a mandarin?

A breed apart

Selective breeding, also known as **artificial selection**, is used to develop hybrid organisms with features we find desirable. Scientists select two foods, each with their own beneficial qualities, to reproduce and they in turn produce offspring with those characteristics. Selective breeding can be used to produce tastier fruits and vegetables, as well as crops with greater tolerance to insects.

SCIENCE CHALLENGE

If you could use artificial selection to create your own hybrid fruit or vegetable, what would you make? Draw a picture of your new selectively bred food and make a list of its special qualities!

Purple patch

Did you know that carrots haven't always been orange? Originally, natural carrots were either white or purple, and they were mostly inedible. Since then, carrots have been selectively bred to improve both their flavour and colour.

Eat your greens

Broccoli isn't a hybrid, but the result of selectively breeding wild cabbage for hundreds of years. Broccoli has been adapted over time to be more delicious and enjoyable for humans! Cabbage, cauliflower, brussels sprouts and kale are all vegetables derived from the same wild cabbage as broccoli. Talk about an overachiever!

Technically speaking, all fruits and vegetables are actually hybrids. If you go back in time far enough, all plants were created thanks to the wind and bees combining different pollens and seeds. We humans have just added to the mix with our selective breeding!

THE MAN WHO SAVED A BILLION LIVES

Have you ever heard of the plant scientist **Norman Borlaug**? Don't worry, not a lot of people have! But you'd think that the man who won a Nobel Peace Prize, was considered the father of the green revolution, and whose work helped save as many as one billion people from starvation would be a household name around the world!

Little wonders

During his career, Dr Borlaug developed new wheat plants which were smaller, less likely to get diseases and could produce higher yields. This new breeding technique was embraced by farmers in Mexico and Asia. The new wheat plants increased food production, and helped to avoid predicted mass famines and save many millions from hunger. Dr Borlaug and his wheat plants literally altered the course of history. What a guy!

Grass roots

Wheat is a type of grass which is widely cultivated for its seed. It's the **third most produced** cereal crop in the world! Wheat provides approximately **20%** of the protein requirements for **more than half** of the world's population.

The greatest

Dr Borlaug has saved more lives than any other person who has ever lived! That's a pretty good reason for him to become a household name!

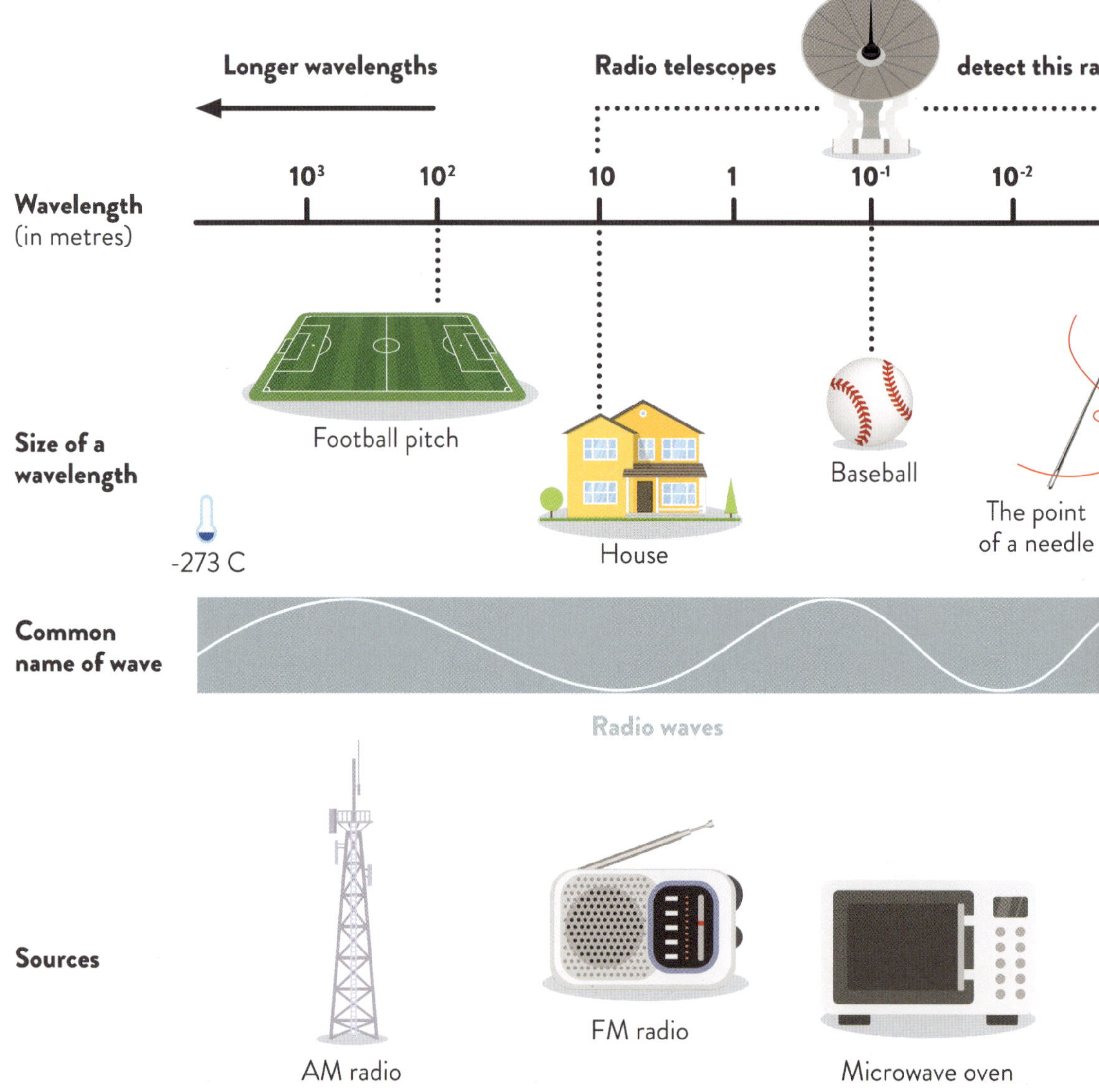

MOST TYPES OF LIGHT ARE INVISIBLE TO OUR EYES

The **electromagnetic spectrum** is the range that describes all of the different kinds of lights there are, including those that are invisible to our human eyes! If you've ever seen a rainbow then you know the different colours that make up the light we can see, but these are only a very small part of the **electromagnetic spectrum**. Amazingly, most of the light in the universe is made of things the human eye can't see. These other types of light include **radio waves**, **microwaves**, **infrared radiation**, **ultraviolet rays**, **X-rays** and **gamma rays**.

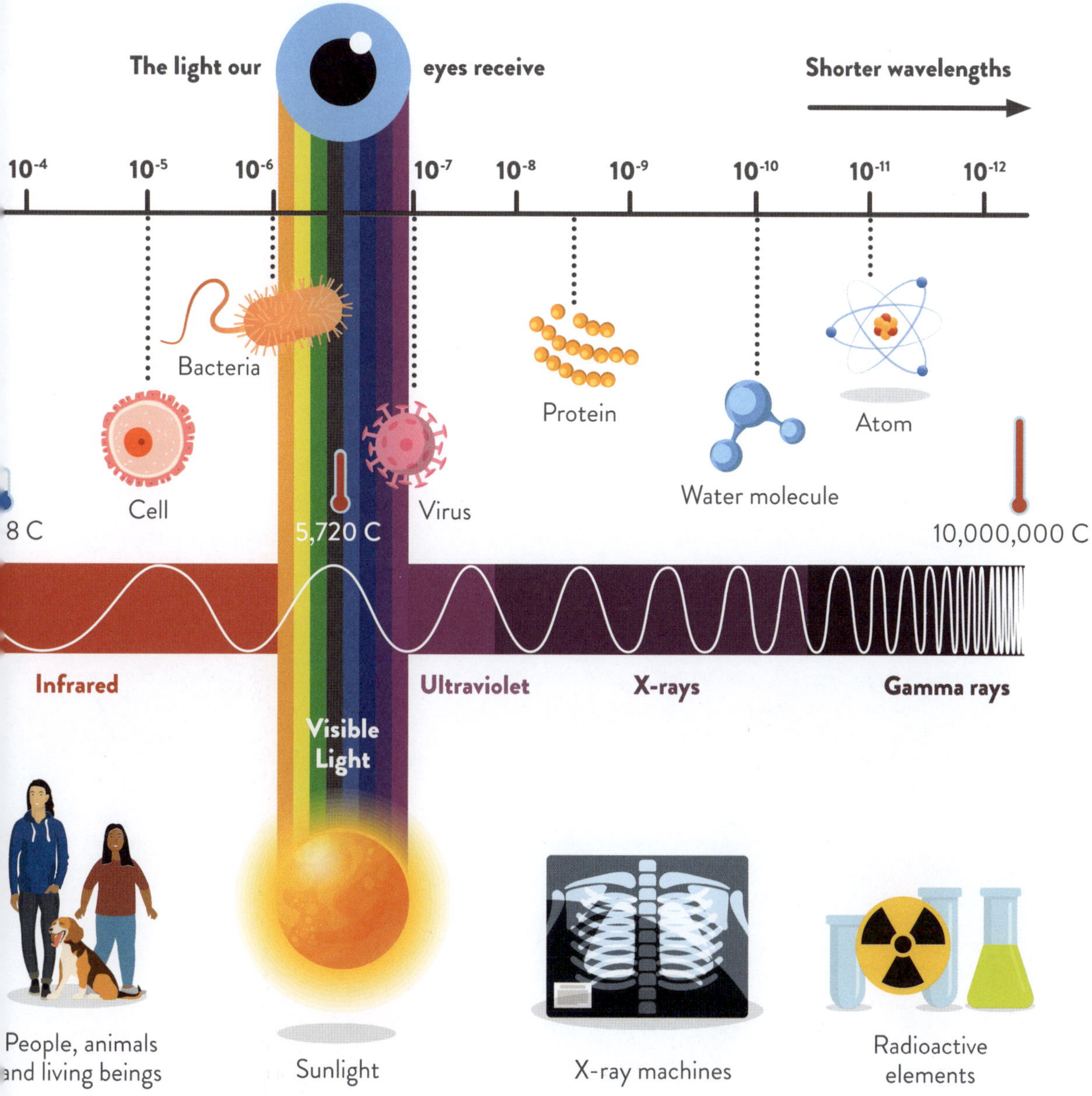

The light our eyes receive

Shorter wavelengths

10^{-4} 10^{-5} 10^{-6} 10^{-7} 10^{-8} 10^{-9} 10^{-10} 10^{-11} 10^{-12}

Bacteria

Cell

Protein

Atom

Virus

Water molecule

8 C

5,720 C

10,000,000 C

Infrared

Ultraviolet

X-rays

Gamma rays

Visible Light

People, animals and living beings

Sunlight

X-ray machines

Radioactive elements

Filter out

Although ultraviolet light is invisible to us, there are some people who report being able to see it. Normally the lens in our eye filters out the ultraviolet light, but some people who are born without a lens (and have not had it replaced) claim they are able to see ultraviolet. To them the world looks very different, with an additional whitish-violet light everywhere.

HEAVY OBJECTS DISTORT THE FABRIC OF SPACE AND TIME

It was the legendary **Sir Isaac Newton** who discovered that gravity is a force of attraction, pulling together everything in the universe. The strength of a gravitational pull depends on how large and close one object is to another. For example, the Sun has a lot more gravity than Earth, but rather than everything living on Earth being pulled towards the Sun, we stay put because of our proximity to the planet's surface.

Stroke of genius

Newton told us what gravity is, but to figure out how it works we needed another genius, Albert Einstein. As it turns out, gravity wasn't a force as Newton had supposed, but something far stranger than that! With his **General Theory of Relativity**, Einstein developed a mind-blowing new way to describe gravity and what causes it.

Einstein concluded that gravity is a natural consequence of a mass's distortion on space and time itself. In his theory, he expressed this as **spacetime**. Every object distorts the fabric of spacetime, and the bigger the object, the greater the effect. It may sound confusing, but all this basically means is that an object can warp, bend, push or pull the spacetime around them, and the extent of this change depending on the size of the object itself.

Time warp

If you placed a bowling ball on a rubber sheet it would stretch the material, and that's exactly how planets and stars warp space-time. A marble rolling along that same rubber sheet would be drawn towards the bowling ball. In the same way, planets orbiting the Sun aren't actually being attracted by it, but they're following the curved space-time deformation caused by the star's massive weight. The reason the planets don't fall into the Sun is because they have a lot of sideways momentum, meaning they're continually falling towards the Sun, but just miss it.

WE MIGHT BE LIVING IN A COMPUTER SIMULATION

Simulation theory is the idea that humans are all digital-beings, and we live inside a computer simulation created by our technologically advanced future descendants. Although this sounds like the bonkers plot from a sci-fi film, it's something many scientists take seriously!

Mind blowing

There are two main parts to the argument that we are, in fact, living inside a computer simulation. The first requires a huge leap of the imagination and asks us to accept that at some point in the future, we'll be able to simulate human consciousness inside a computer in a way which makes it indistinguishable from real human consciousnes. This is called **ancestor simulations**.

Powerhouse

The second part of the argument is that any future civilisation would need to have monumental amounts of computing power at their disposal, dwarfing anything we have today. They could then use this advanced processing power to run the ancestor simulations.

Question marks

If it turns out that we are actually living in a computer simulation, it still leaves a huge question unanswered. Where did the original, non-simulated world come from? And then there's the question of what would happen if we invented our own ancestor simulation that nests inside our reality? Or has this already happened many times over?

SMALLPOX IS THE ONLY DISEASE HUMANS HAVE EVER WIPED OUT

Smallpox was once a highly contagious and fatal disease. Before 1980 smallpox was regarded as one of the world's deadliest diseases, killing **3 out of every 10 infected people**. But thanks to public health efforts and a worldwide immunisation project we finally managed to wipe it out!

This was the first and only time humans have managed to fully get rid of a human disease. Overall, smallpox caused the deaths of **hundreds of millions** of people before we stopped it for good. Go science!

MILLION

This is the estimated number of people around the world who died from smallpox in the 20th century.

Tailor-made solution

The vaccine for smallpox was discovered thanks to an 18th-century English scientist called **Edward Jenner**. Jenner noticed that milkmaids who had a mild disease called **'cowpox'** seemed immune to smallpox! He used cowpox in his vaccination against smallpox, and eventually a virus similar to cowpox called **'vaccinia'** was substituted in the vaccine. This is the origin of the word **vaccination**.

Mum's the word

Smallpox has been around ever since humans have recorded history. There are even Egyptian mummies with tell-tale pockmarked skin!

Weapons of mass destruction

Even though smallpox is now gone there is always the chance it could return – some people even fear that it could be used as a biological weapon. The United States has stockpiled enough of the vaccine to inoculate every single one of its citizens, just in case.

YOU CAN TRAP A

Lasers are brilliant, and easily one of the best things in all of science! They're super powerful, amazingly versatile and have the ability to travel across huge distances. Not to mention they look pretty cool! It might surprise you to learn that, for all the power a laser has, it's actually very easy to trap a laser beam in water. And what's more, you can do this at home. Easy peasy!

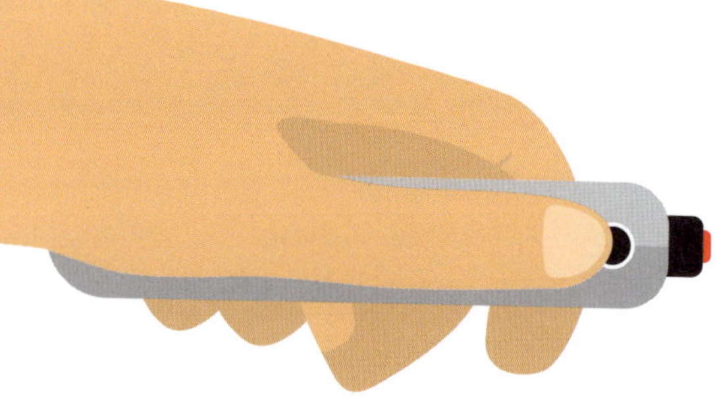

Caught in a trap

To trap your laser, you will need a laser pointer and a large plastic bottle full of water. Take the bottle and poke a hole in the side, letting a stream of water arc out of the hole. Aim the laser pointer through the bottle and watch as it gets trapped within the waterfall you've created, arching downwards with the water's flow!

LASER IN WATER

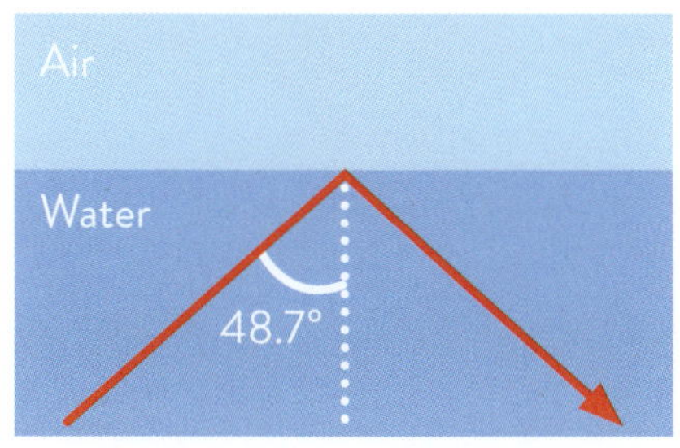

Upon reflection

When the beam of light from the laser hits the edge of the waterspout at a certain angle, it's forced to reflect rather than passing right through it. This reflection happens over and over again as the light repeatedly hits the edge, causing the laser to remain trapped in the waterfall. This process is called **total internal reflection**.

Playing the angles

In order for total internal reflection to occur, the light must be inside a denser medium as it moves towards the boundary of a less dense medium – in this case water and air.

The light must also hit the boundary at an angle greater than the 'critical angle' – for water and air this angle is **48.6°**. Once the angle increases above this the light is reflected back.

Fibre optics

The cables that give you your speedy internet also use total internal reflection. Optical-fibre cables are made up of long fibres of glass or plastic that trap the beams of light inside.

Think tank

You can also witness total internal reflection in a glass tank full of water! Send the beam at just the right angle and it will bounce off the water's surface and back into the tank before bouncing off the bottom and out again!

ONLY 9% OF THE WORLD'S PLASTIC IS RECYCLED

We are surrounded by plastic. This lightweight, tough, waterproof and synthetic material has played a huge role in all human lives over the past **100 years**. But it's in those years that it has gone from being celebrated as a scientific marvel to being hated as an environmental menace.

Plastic's advantage as a long-lasting material became its greatest disadvantage. Plastic might sit in a landfill, litter a street or float in an ocean for thousands of years without decomposing. While we do recycle plastic, the increasingly massive numbers of production (half of all plastic that has ever existed was made in the past 13 years) means that **91%** of all plastics remain unrecycled.

Go fish

It's estimated that by **2050** the ocean will contain more plastic by weight than fish.

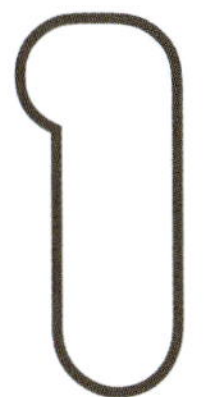

MILLION

The number of plastic bottles bought around the world every single minute.

The number of years that plastic bottles take to decompose.

TRILLION

The number of kilograms of plastic that humans have produced since 1950, of which, **6.3 trillion kilograms** have become waste.

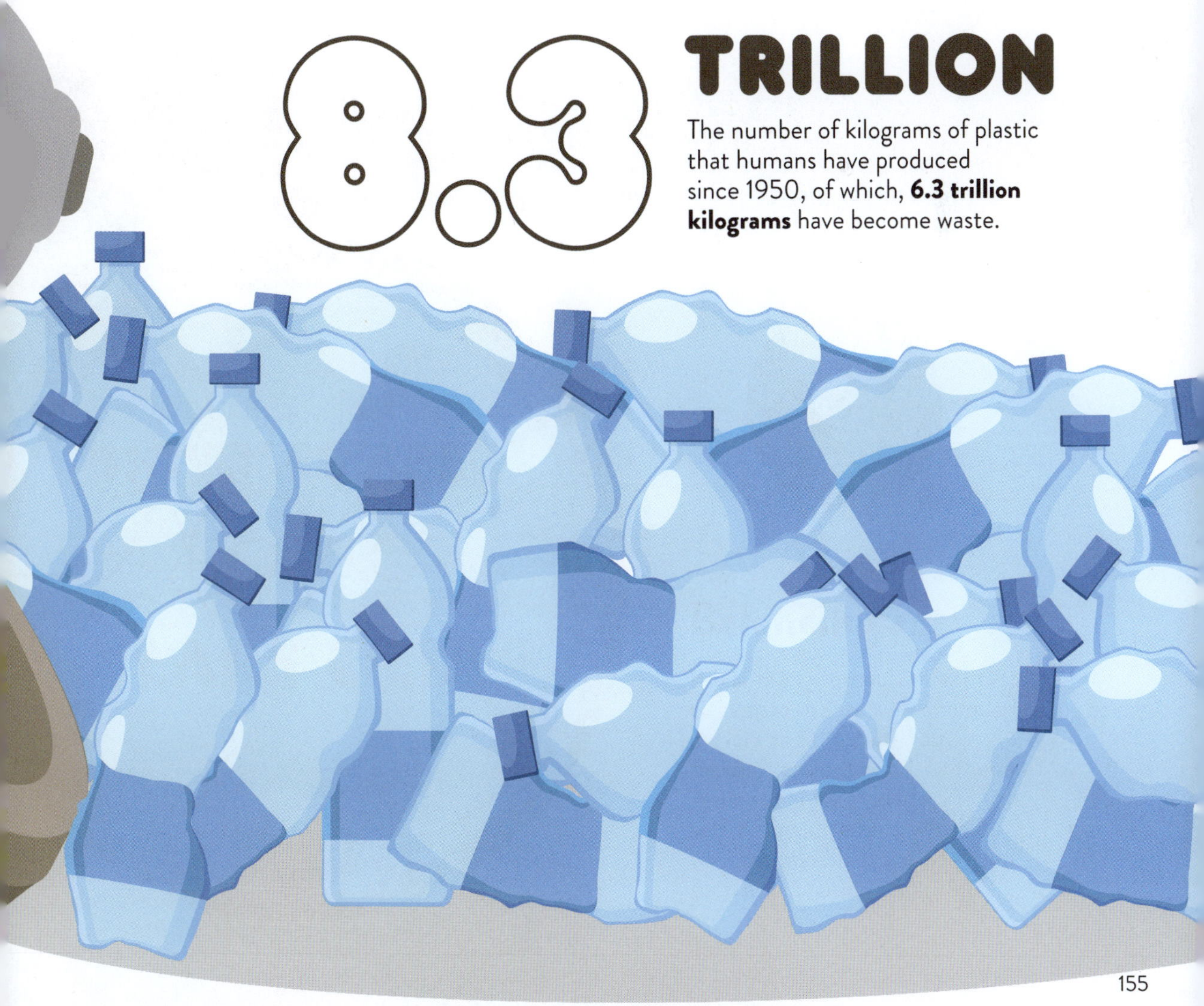

VIRUSES CAN GET VIRUSES

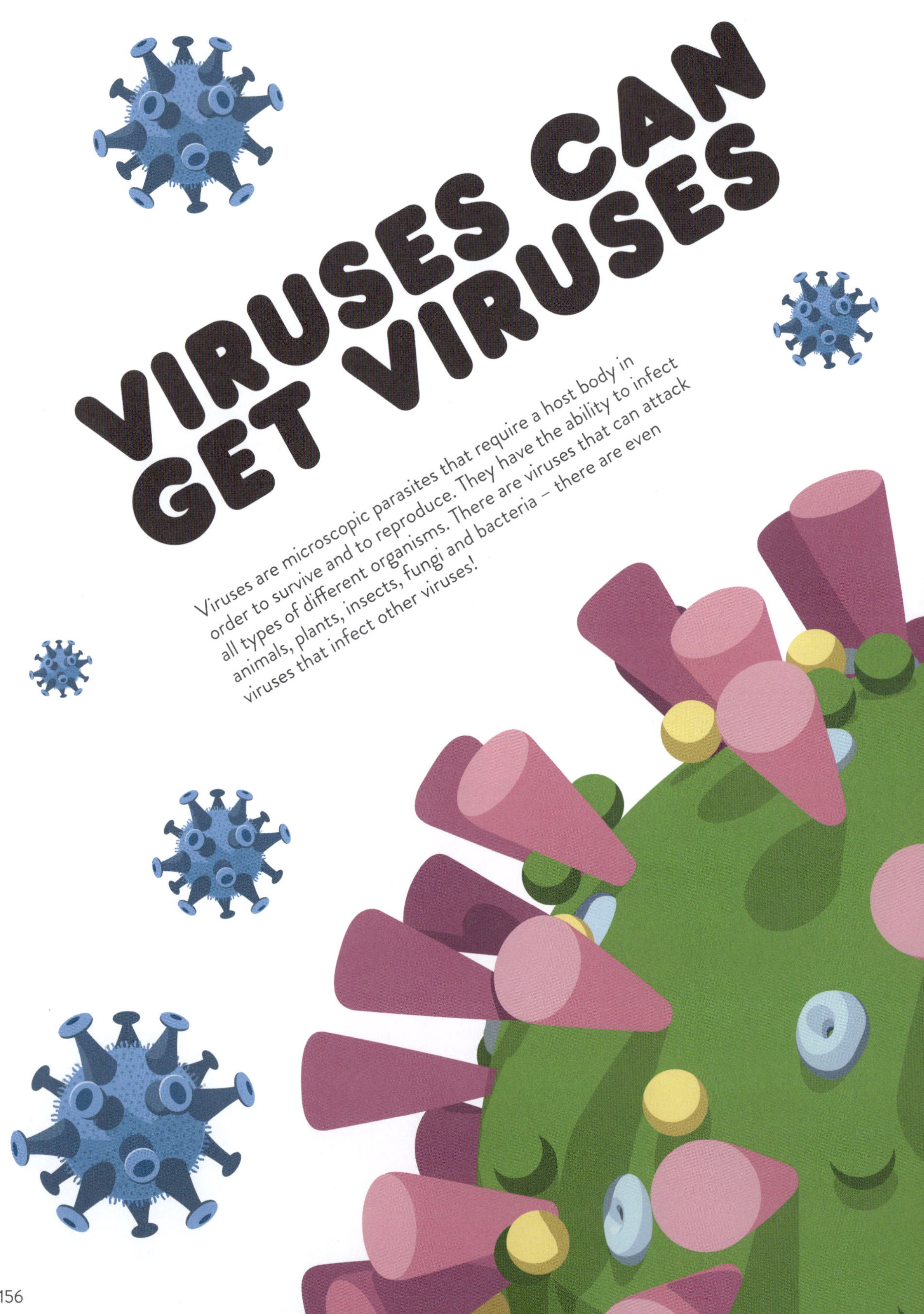

Viruses are microscopic parasites that require a host body in order to survive and to reproduce. They have the ability to infect all types of different organisms. There are viruses that can attack animals, plants, insects, fungi and bacteria – there are even viruses that infect other viruses!

Gone viral

A tiny virus that is a parasite of another larger virus has been discovered for the first time. This tiny virus causes trouble when it reproduces in a cell already inhabited by a larger virus, which causes it to get sick!

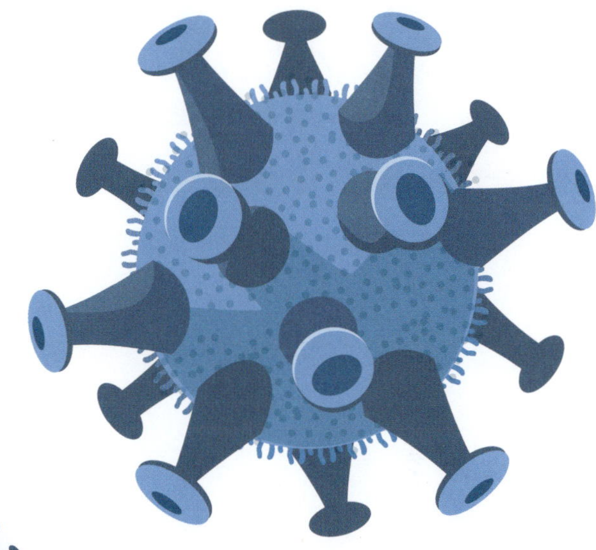

Alive and kicking

Because viruses do not share common characteristics with other forms of life, they're not considered to be alive. But the discovery that one virus can infect another is making scientists question that!

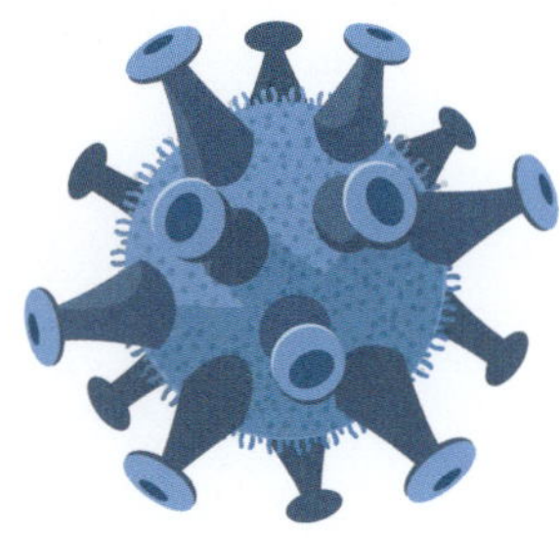

YOU CAN START A FIRE WITH ICE

Fire and water don't make for the most obvious of companions. So, it may fascinate you to learn that you can actually use some frozen water to start a fire! And it's a much simpler a process than you might think: all you need is some clear ice, direct sunshine and your own two hands.

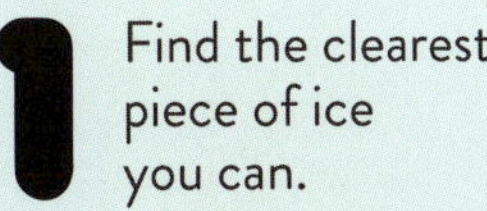

1 Find the clearest piece of ice you can.

2 Using your hands, begin to thin the outside of the ice by melting it.

3 Once the ice is thinned, mould it into a smooth-edged circular shape like a magnifying glass.

If you decide to try to make fire from ice **always let an adult know what you are doing** and have them supervise you. It's important to light your fire in a safe place, and make sure that you only focus your magnifying ice on your tinder!

4 Concentrate the sunlight with your ice onto some tinder, being extra careful not to get any water drops on it. Wait patiently and then eventually you will have ignition. You just made fire from ice!

LIGHT HAS NO SHADOW

A shadow is a dark area created around an object whenever light is unable to travel through it. If you look around, you'll see shadows absolutely everywhere! From tables to toys and trees to termites, any object (living or not) can cast a shadow.

But you'll be surprised by the one thing that does not cast a shadow. Light! This is because light cannot block light. In fact, if you were to shine a light on light then all you'd be doing is adding to the intensity of the first light, helping it to grow brighter still.

SCIENCE CHALLENGE

Make your own sundial out of a paper plate and a pencil. Draw a clockface with twelve evenly spaced numbers and insert the pencil in the middle of the plate so that it stands tall. On a sunny day, take your sundial outside, place it on a flat surface and make sure that it faces due south. The shadow from the pencil will fall on the time. Ta-da!

Dial up

In the past, we used the shadows cast by the Sun to develop the world's first ever clocks, called **sundials**. We don't know who invented them, but they are one of the oldest scientific instruments of the world.

Size up

As well as being used as early time-keeping devices, shadows were also used to first accurately calculate the size of the Earth. Over **2000 years ago**, **Eratosthenes** was able to combine simple geometry and shadow measurements to first perform this incredible task!

ANI

APES AND MONKEYS HAVE ENTERED THE STONE AGE

For humans, the Stone Age was a period of pre-history in which we used primitive stone tools. We did this for roughly **2.5 million years**, until **5000 years ago** we began working with metal, making tools and weapons from bronze. But for the tiny white-faced Capuchin monkeys, their own Stone Age is currently happening! They are known to use stone tools daily, and often save stones for repeated use, something they have been doing for over **3000 years**!

Hammer home

Humans have been using stones as hammers and anvils for at least **3 million years**, and now these little monkeys are using large stones, which are almost half their body weight, to smash open shellfish, nuts and other foods.

Monkey business

Chimpanzees have an entire tool kit that includes stone hammers, shovel-like branches used to drill holes into termite nests, and straw probes to remove the tasty insect treats inside.

MILLION

The number of years of evolution that separates humans from the Capuchin monkey.

Aping around

As well as using sticks to probe logs for honey, Orangutans are also amazing engineers who are capable of building elaborate nests that would impress any human architect!

THE MANTIS SHRIMP HAS THE FASTEST AND MOST POWERFUL PUNCH IN THE WORLD

Mantis shrimps may be small (typically about **10 centimetres in length**) but these little powerhouses can punch at **80 kilometres per hour**, landing a blow with the same force as a bullet! This punch would definitely leave some imaginary birds chirping around your head!

Pack a punch

What is even more mind-blowing is that this stunning punch is thrown in water, managing to move rapidly through considerable drag and resistance. Nothing can get in the mantis shrimp's way as it delivers its thunderous wallop in **three thousandths of a second**.

Boiling point

The shrimp's power and speed come from the large muscles in its upper arm, which fire like a spring, accelerating at up to **10,000 times the force of gravity**! The shrimp's arm moves through the water so quickly that it lowers the pressure and pushes the water to boiling point, producing flashes of light.

Cracking up

These tough-guy crustaceans use their power to feast on crabs, snails and small fish, but are known to take on large fish, and even the occasional octopus! They also have a reputation for cracking aquarium glass and damaging boats. The mantis shrimp is one little fighter you do not want to mess with!

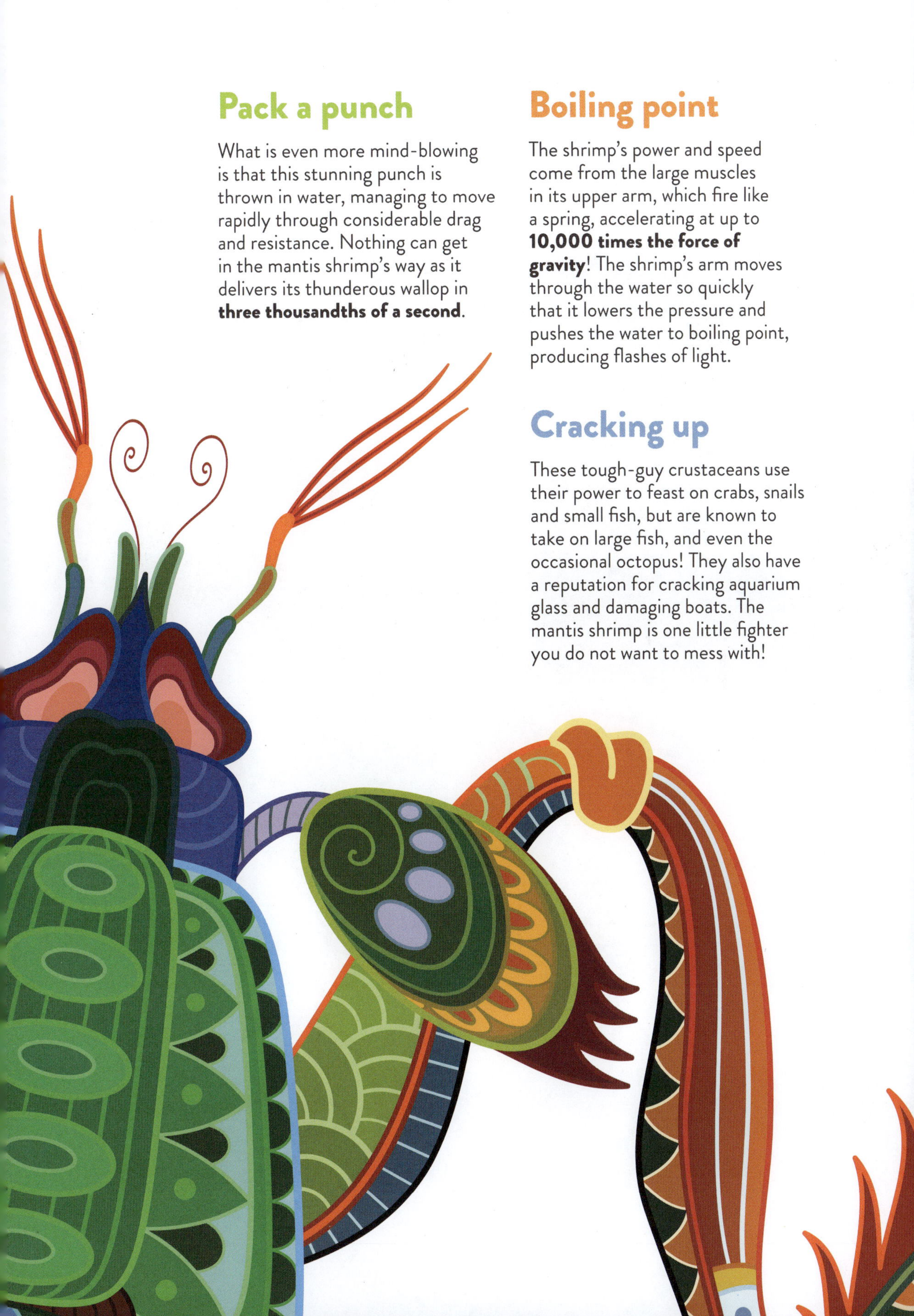

BEES CAN SEE THE INVISIBLE

Bees see the world very differently to how humans do. This is because bees are able to see light on a spectrum that is invisible to us – the **ultraviolet spectrum**. If humans were to see the world as a bee, we would see a landing strip when we looked at plants. These landing strips guide bees to the plant's nectar, which they then feed on.

The feeling is mutual

Bees and flowering plants have a relationship that is described as **mutualistic**, which means they both benefit from it. The flowers provide the bee with nectar and pollen, which they collect and take back to their colonies for food. In exchange, the bees help the flowers to reproduce, as when the bee flies from flower to flower they spread the pollen they've collected in a process called **pollination**.

Once in a lifetime

On average a worker bee will only produce **one twelfth of a teaspoon of honey** in their entire lifetime! It takes the full working-life of **12 worker bees** to produce just a single teaspoon of honey.

The royal treatment

A queen bee can produce **2000 eggs** in a single day! The queen bee uses her pheromones to instruct the workers on which eggs should be fertilised and which shouldn't. The fertilised eggs become female bees, and unfertilised eggs become males! Queen honeybees can live up to **5 years**, much longer than her worker bees who only live for **5–6 weeks**. Tough life.

Honey is more amazing than you probably realise. If honey is sealed in an airtight container it will last forever. Did you know that archaeologists have even found honey that's **several thousand years old** in Egyptian tombs?

Song and dance

Honeybees are able to communicate with each other using physical movements. Bees have been known to headbutt each other when they're trying to say 'buzz off'. When scout bees find a new potential home, they do a waggle dance to tell the other scout bees where the nest is!

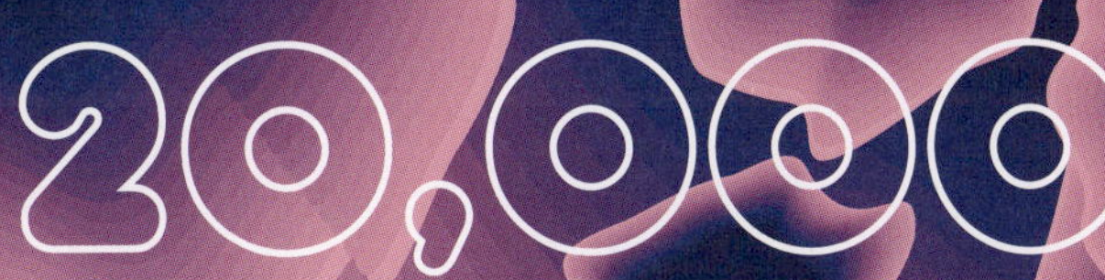

This is the number of different species of bees. Bees are a member of the flying insect family, which includes honeybees, bumblebees and many other fly and wasp-like creatures.

Bread and butter

Bees are commonly associated with making honey, but that's not all they make! Bees build honeycomb structures by secreting beeswax from their glands, and they also make an edible blend of pollen and honey, which is their version of bread. As if all this wasn't enough, they also make a gluey substance called **propolis**, which they use to seal up their hives. Busy bees!

THE BRONTOSAURUS IS THE ONLY DINOSAUR TO GO EXTINCT TWICE

Dinosaurs first appeared roughly **245 million years ago** and walked the Earth for nearly **175 million years**. One of these incredible giant reptiles was the Brontosaurus. This famous dinosaur had a very long neck, a huge body and a long whip-like tail. This giant was fairly well-known for gracefully grazing on greens, and living peacefully alongside its fellow animals.

Like almost all dinosaurs, about **66 million years ago** the Brontosaurus became extinct. But you'd be wrong if you thought that's where the story of the Brontosaurus ended! In 1879 its bones were first discovered by famous palaeontologist Othniel Charles Marsh, and he named the dinosaur Brontosaurus (meaning **thunder lizard**).

After the discovery of the Brontosaurus, scientists concluded that they were too similar to another long-necked dinosaur, the **Apatosaurus**, to fully deserve their own title. But recent scientific findings have once again proposed that the Brontosaurus may indeed be its own dinosaur. This decision means that the Brontosaurus is the only dinosaur ever to come back from extinction.

Bird brains

Did you know that birds are actually dinosaurs? They are the sole survivors of the entire dinosaur family tree! Birds not only evolved from meat-eating dinosaurs, but they've thrived while doing so, evolving into **10,000 different species**! If you want a real-life dinosaur encounter take a good look at a chicken – our egg-laying friends are the closest thing to a T-Rex we'll ever see in the flesh!

Stone the crows

Brontosauruses were herbivores, meaning they ate plants. As you can imagine, a dinosaur this big had to eat in large amounts! Because Brontosauruses didn't chew, scientists believe they swallowed whole stones, which then sat undigested in their guts. But it's not all bad, the stones in their bellies helped those thunder lizards to digest the large amounts of plants they had eaten.

ANIMALS CHALLENGE

Look closely at a chicken and a reconstructed image of a T-Rex. Can you draw the two side-by-side and see their familial resemblance? Their clawed feet are a good starting point.

Spiders are in the top class of predators; they're built for killing and survival.

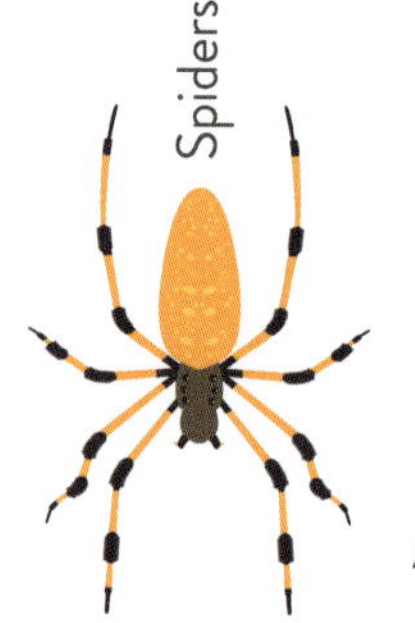

All spiders produce silk. This strong and flexible fibre is **five times stronger** than steel.

As a group, spiders eat more insects than both birds and bats combined.

Spiders locate their captured prey by sensing the vibrations in the silk strands in their web.

Spiders have existed for **400 million years.**

The Goliath birdeater spider has a leg span of almost **30 centimetres.**

SPIDERS COULD EAT EVERY HUMAN ON EARTH IN JUST ONE YEAR

If you're afraid of spiders, now is the time to stop reading! Collectively our eight-legged arachnid friends consume between **400 billion** and **800 billion kilograms of prey every year**. The total weight of all humans on Earth is around **350 billion kilograms** so we'd better hope that the world's spiders don't team up and discuss their dinner options anytime soon. If they wanted to, those web-spinners could feast on every single one of us, and still be hungry for more!

There are spiders that go fishing! They swim, dive and even walk on the water's surface.

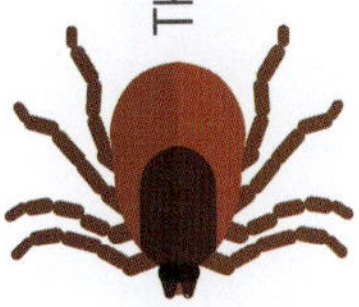

Some spiders fire blobs of silk as a weapon.

In the right conditions, there can be **1000 individual spiders per square metre.**

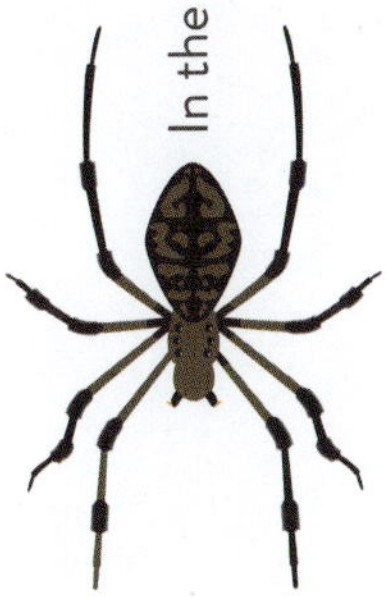

There are over **45,000 different species** of spiders.

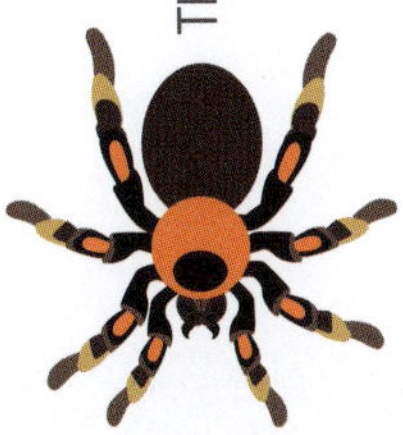

Spiders have external skeletons, also known as **exoskeletons.**

Not all spiders are meat eaters. The Bagheera kiplingi is a mostly plant-eating species.

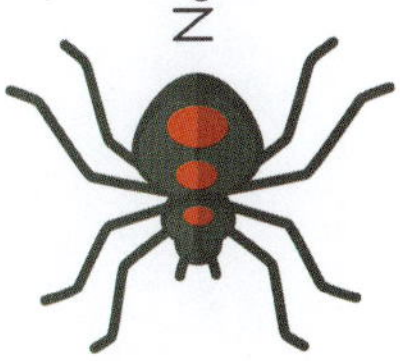

Suck it up

Many species of spider are meat eaters. Most spiders use their webs to trap flies and other insects, but some prefer to hunt their prey. Things get pretty gross once a spider has caught its prey. The spider injects their dinner with digestive fluids, as they're unable to swallow their food as is. Once the digestive fluids have done their work, the spiders suck out the remains like a pre-digested slushie!

Up, up and away

When spiders aren't busy liquifying their prey, they like to catch the wind and electric field with their silk threads and become airborne! This is called **'ballooning'** or **'kiting'**, and sailors have even reported spiders being caught in their ship's sails over **1600 kilometres** from land. But that's not even the craziest part – spiders have even been detected in atmospheric data balloons, which sit around **5 kilometres** above sea level.

ONE IN EVERY ON EARTH IS

There are a *lot* of beetles about. These insects make up a **quarter of all the animal species** humans have discovered. So far, we have found and described over **400,000 different types of beetles**, but we suspect that there may be as many as **3 million** of them out there! Beetles don't just dominate the animal kingdom; they also make up between **one fifth** and **one third** of all the types of life on Earth that we've so far managed to describe. The undeniable success of the humble beetle is all because of the way they have evolved to perform extremely varied and specific roles, from pollinating trees to eating animal dung. Not glamourous, but very effective!

40%

This is the amount of all the insect species we have discovered and described that are beetles.

Survivors

The beetles we recognise today have existed for **270 million years.** This means that they were scurrying around the Earth before dinosaurs. It also means that whatever killed the dinosaurs couldn't kill these tough little cookies. For millions of years, the beetle somehow managed to adapt and to survive.

Can you spot the **five ladybugs** among the many beetles on this page?

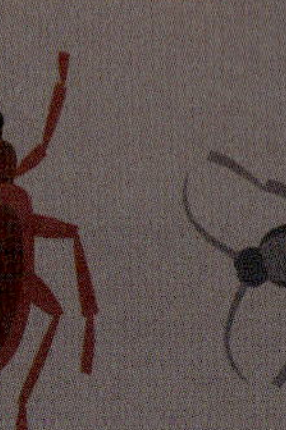

FOUR ANIMALS BEETLE

Winging it

Beetles have not just one, but two pairs of wings! The first pair are hardened wing cases that protect the second pair, which are used for flying.

Here, there and everywhere

Beetles live just about everywhere on the planet, but the only place we haven't found them is on the ice of the polar regions and in the saltwater of the oceans.

Tiger king

Relative to its size, the **tiger beetle** is the fastest creature on Earth. These beetles can run at a speed of **9 kilometres per hour**, which is **125 times** their own body length in a single second! For comparison, humans can only run about **five times** their own body length in that time. To beat the tiger beetle in a race, a person would have to run **770 kilometres per hour**!

YOU'RE MORE LIKELY TO BE KILLED BY A VENDING MACHINE THAN BY A SHARK

Sharks have a terrifying reputation as fierce ocean-dwelling predators who would gobble you up as soon as you dipped your little toe in the ocean. But, if you look at the statistics of deaths by shark attacks, that's a pretty unfair reputation. In fact, every year vending machines kill more people than sharks do, usually by falling on top of someone as they angrily try to shake their food and drink out.

Dancing with death

It isn't just vending machines that are more deadly than sharks. We're in more danger of being killed by falling coconuts, champagne corks, beds, ladders, hippopotamuses and mosquitos. Every year there are:

10

deaths worldwide from shark attacks.

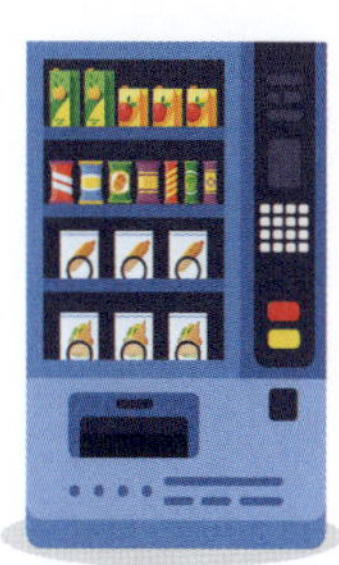

13

deaths worldwide from vending machines.

150

deaths worldwide from falling coconuts.

450

deaths in the United States from falling out of bed.

24

deaths worldwide from flying champagne corks.

355

deaths in the United States caused by falling off ladders.

500

deaths in Africa from being attacked by a hippopotamus.

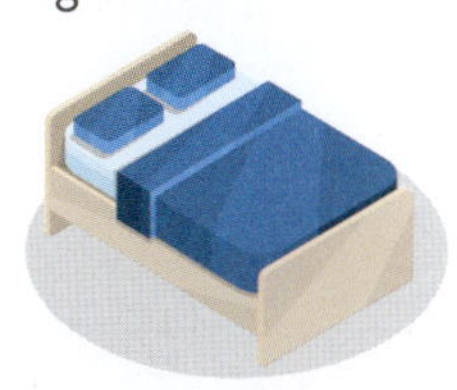

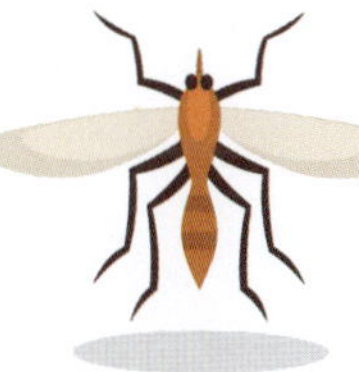

830,000

deaths worldwide from mosquitos carrying malaria, Zika, dengue fever, Japanese encephalitis and yellow fever.

Killing off

Considering they only kill **10** of us annually, it seems horrifying that every year humans kill an estimated **100 million** sharks – some estimates put that number closer to **300 million**! If we use the lower estimate of **100 million**, that would mean there are **11,416 sharks** killed by humans **every single hour**.

Old timers

Sharks may have been terrifying humans for a long time, but they've been swimming in Earth's oceans for a lot longer still – **450 million years**, to be precise. That's **230 million years** before the dinosaurs! Sharks are even older than trees, which first appeared as developing forests on Earth **370 million years ago**.

CATS ONLY MEOW AT HUMANS

It's easy to assume that the loud and repeated meowing of a domestic cat as it demands to be fed is a sound it makes to communicate with humans and cats alike. But the reality is that adult cats very rarely, if ever, meow at one another – that's something they reserve for chatting with humans. Lucky us!

Kittens do meow to their mothers to gain their attention, but once they grow up they stop meowing to other cats. Cats that live with humans use 'baby behaviour' towards their owners because we respond to it – in fact, sometimes we even talk back to them in a different, higher-pitched voice.

Let's talk

As well as meowing, there are around **100 other cat noises** that our furry friends use to communicate with us. Among them are purring, trilling, growling, chattering, hissing, yowling, beeping, burbling and wailing.

Heads and tails

As well as verbally communicating, cats also use their ears, eyes, body position and, most importantly, their tails to tell you their mood and what they are thinking.

A cat's tail can move incredibly quickly or slowly in a whole variety of positions. They can even bristle their hair outwards as they hold their tails aloft, which means they are very angry!

DOLPHINS ARE NO

Dolphins are highly intelligent. They've even been called as clever as humans – possibly even more so, depending on who you're talking about! Like us, dolphins can recognise themselves in a mirror, which is a sign of self-awareness and something that most other animals can't do. They're also completely aware of their body parts, and understand that they are in charge of their own movements, while simultaneously having emotions and displaying self-control. Besides these similarities, dolphins are clearly intelligent in different ways too, which is perhaps why we should treat them as our evolutionary equals. It seems that dolphins are 'people' just like us, they're just happy to live in the water.

Good grief

Dolphins also seem to be aware of the cycle of life, and mourn those who have passed away. In what appears to be a grieving ceremony, they support the body of a dead dolphin on top of the ocean, normally for half an hour or so, but sometimes this ceremony can last for days!

I know what you're thinking

Dolphins form tight social groups and cliques. In fact, these groups are so close that it has led some scientists to suggest that there is a form of telepathy occurring between dolphins.

Signature style

Dolphins are capable of a type of verbal communication that closely resembles how humans speak. Dolphins use a highly developed series of whistles, clicks and buzzing and pulsing sounds to communicate with each other. Each dolphin has its own signature whistle, which acts like a name for it.

Make it official

In India, dolphins are officially recognised as non-human persons whose rights to life and freedom must always be respected.

-HUMAN PEOPLE

PIGS CAN'T LOOK UP

Pigs have an amazing sense of smell, one that's almost **2000 times more sensitive** than a human's! This super sense of smell is why you often see pigs with their snouts to the ground, sniffing and digging in the dirt, foraging for food.

This fantastic gift of smell also gives pigs a huge physical disadvantage. Pigs are unable to raise their heads above 15°, which means that they can lift their heads a little bit, but not enough to gaze up at the clouds in the sky. Instead of looking up, pigs are able to lift themselves up on their front legs to see higher, or to lie on their backs and look upwards. But don't worry, pigs don't seem to mind, as they're generally more interested in finding their next delicious treat on the ground.

ANIMALS CHALLENGE

Use a compass or a protractor to measure 15°. Pretend to be a pig and look no higher than that to see exactly how limiting it is to have the gaze of a pig!

Social network

Pigs are very social animals, forming very close bonds with different pigs and with other animals. Pigs are such good friends that they even like to cuddle up with one another to keep warm.

Smart cookies

Just because they can't look up doesn't mean that pigs aren't smart. Pigs are considered one of the most intelligent animals – they're able to outsmart dogs and chimpanzees! We think pigs have the same intelligence level as a 2-year-old human.

2 BILLION

This is the total population of pigs in the world. In Denmark there are **6 million people** and almost **18 million pigs**. That's **three times as many pigs** as there are people!

Pigs are highly social and very vocal, using their grunts to communicate with each other. A pig's grunt lets others know their wellbeing, and the grunts can vary depending on the personality of the pig.

OWLS HAVE LONG LEGS

So many things in the animal world are not what they first appear, and owls are no exception. Did you know that if you were to lift up an owl's bottom feathers you would find a pair of very long, skinny legs?

Down in one

Owls have no teeth so they swallow their prey whole. Fur, skin, bones ... the lot.

Leg work

Owls are incredible hunters, and their powerful grip comes from the strength of their leg muscles. Their long legs are what help them to catch their prey!

Get a grip

Owls are **zygodactyl**. This means that their feet have two middle toes that face forwards and two outer toes that face backwards. This allows them to firmly grip their prey. However, unlike other birds that are zygodactyl, owls can move one toe from the back to the front, allowing them to walk and perch.

THE LARGEST ANIMAL THAT'S EVER LIVED CANNOT SWALLOW ANYTHING BIGGER THAN A GRAPEFRUIT

Blue whales are the undisputed kings of the ocean. They are **three times the size** of the largest dinosaurs of the land and sea, and bigger than any other creature alive today. You'd think that a creature so massive would be feasting on similarly enormous food, but that's not the case.

Despite their size, the throat of a blue whale is tiny, which stops it from devouring anything larger than a grapefruit. But when a blue whale eats, it definitely eats in quantity!

Snack attack

The blue whale's food of choice is **krill**. These miniature, pink, shrimp-like creatures slip down the whale's slim gullet with remarkable ease. These whale snacks like to swarm in belly-filling numbers, with some mobs weighing in at a hefty **90 million kilograms** – that's roughly equivalent to **643 blue whales**!

Feeding frenzy

When travelling and breeding, blue whales can sometimes endure **6–8 months** of near starvation. As you'd expect, when these peckish whales find their way back to waters where krill are plentiful, they don't hold back. During their feeding season, blue whales can gorge on more than **40 million krill** in a single day. That's around **4000 kilograms** of food!

Wide open

To chow down on such monstrous hordes of krill, blue whales swim with their massive mouths wide open, swallowing their gargantuan shrimp cocktails whole. In the process, they also take in huge amounts of water, which they filter out with their **2700-kilogram tongues**.

EVERY MODERN-DAY DOG SHARES A COMMON ANCESTOR WITH THE GREY WOLF

You only have to spend five minutes in a dog park to see that man's best friend comes in the most spectacular array of shapes, sizes, colours and coats. In fact, there are over **340 different breeds** of dog! It's pretty extraordinary that all these different breeds share a single common ancestor with ***Canis lupus***, the grey wolf.

Domestic bliss

Scientists believe dogs' common ancestor was a prehistoric wolf that lived in Europe or Asia as long as **34,000 years ago**. Dog skulls dating back **33,000 years** have been found in caves which were known to be inhabited by humans. This evidence indicates that dogs were the first species to be domesticated, and had begun evolving along with us before humans even invented agriculture!

Smart cookies

The reasons these pooches became domesticated is still unclear. One theory is that the dogs' wolfy ancestors befriended human hunter-gatherers by moving near the outskirts of their camps and scavenging for leftover food. The tamer and less aggressive wolves would have been the most successful at this, which would have taught them to behave for their new human friends. Smart cookies.

Besties

It makes sense that our hunter-gatherer ancestors would have developed a symbiotic relationship with wolves; trading their leftover food for help with hunting and scaring away other animals. Over time, this relationship would see those wolves evolve into our modern-day animal besties. In fact, it's our selective breeding of dogs that has contributed to the vast variety of breeds we know today. As we have developed our long relationship with dogs, we have also directly affected their evolution.

ANTS HAVE CONQUERED THE EARTH

As a species, humans can be pretty smug; there's no doubt that we consider ourselves the dominant species on Earth. There are over **7.8 billion** of us, and we've managed to effectively cover the globe, building civilisations and engineering the land to suit our own needs.

But it turns out that another species may already be in charge, only they've kept their dominance on the down low. Ants already control the planet. In terms of population, there are **10,000,000,000,000,000** of them – that's **10,000 trillion** ants! This mind-blowing number works out at **1.3 million** ants per human.

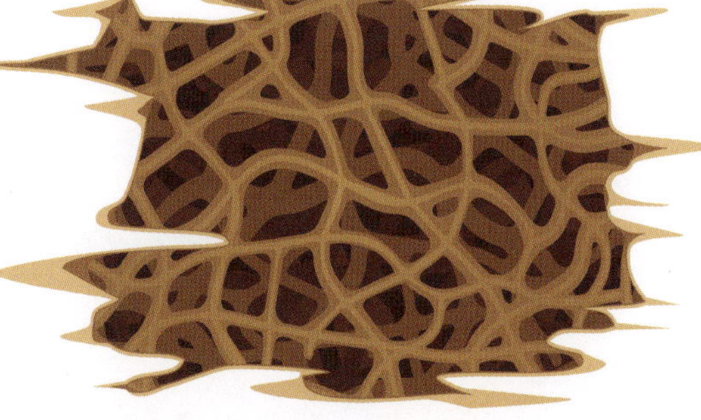

A hive of activity

The ants living beneath our feet are extremely intelligent. Individually, a single ant may not appear to be all that clever, but collaboratively ants can solve extraordinary problems with their hive mind. Like humans, ant colonies have the power to engineer the world around them. They build hugely elaborate and interconnected chambers under the ground – all the while working together and sharing jobs between them.

All things equal

You'd think that humans' superior size would make us the dominant species, right? Wrong. If you compared the collective weight of every ant on the planet and that of every human, you'd find that these two biomasses are about equal.

Extreme behaviour

Not only are ants monumental in numbers, they're also everywhere! Given their ability to survive at the various extremes of the natural world, from the Sahara Desert to near the Arctic Circle, it's no wonder almost every landmass on the planet has ants.

Born survivors

Humans have been on Earth for what seems like an eternity, but our **200,000 years** of existence have nothing on ants, who **130 million years ago** shared the planet with the dinosaurs, and survived the mass extinction that wiped those dinosaurs out! All hail our ant masters!

KOALAS' FINGERPRINTS ARE ALMOST IDENTICAL TO HUMAN ONES

If police ever investigated a crime scene inside the koala enclosure at the zoo, they'd have their work cut out for them. They'd have an extremely hard time telling the difference between any human or koala fingerprints they found there, as our fingerprints are so similar that when viewed under a microscope it's difficult to distinguish between the unique swirling patterns.

Grasping at straws

Koalas aren't the only animals who have unique fingerprints; other close human relatives such as chimpanzees and gorillas have fingerprints too! Our fingerprints are incredibly helpful when it comes to grip, as well as making our touch more sensitive, which allows us to have a more detailed sensory experience when we hold and touch things.

Koalas are very particular about what they eat, with their preferred dinner being eucalyptus leaves of a certain age. Their fingerprints mean that koalas can give their food a really good inspection before they chow down.

Take a close look at the ends of your fingers. Fingerprints are the tiny ridges, whirls and patterns on the tip of each finger. No two individuals with the same fingerprints have ever been found, both for humans and animals alike! Fingerprints are virtually unique, no matter who owns them. But that doesn't mean they are *completely* unique. There's a one in **64 billion** chance that your fingerprint will match up exactly with someone else's!

Leaf through

Koalas have a big appetite and can eat up to **1 kilogram** of eucalyptus leaves a day!

CROWS NEVER FORGET A FACE ...

Make it your mission to never upset a crow. Thanks to their very own internal facial-recognition system, these highly intelligent birds will have you marked down on their naughty list.

Crows have the ability to decipher very complex puzzles, sometimes involving multiple parts that need to be solved in a specific order so they can receive a reward.

Tool up

Crows can even use tools, sometimes combining more than one to achieve their desired result. These brilliant birds have been observed snapping twigs from trees, removing the bark and leaves, and then creating a hook which allows them to probe into small spaces for food!

... AND HOLD GRUDGES

Not only will they be able to recognise you again, but thanks to their amazing memories they will be able to do so for up to **5 years** after you have offended them. And as well as holding this grudge, these crows will tell all their friends about you too!

Shiny, happy people

As well as holding grudges against anyone who upsets them, crows can remember anyone who has been nice to them. They have been known to bring shiny objects as gifts to people who regularly reward them with food. Such good eggs!

Playtime

Like a lot of intelligent animals, crows have a playful nature. They've even been spotted snowboarding on snow-covered roofs using a plastic lid as a board!

COWS HAVE BESTIES

The sight of a herd of cows in a field is often one of serenity and calmness. Cows standing and sitting together peacefully, hanging out and chewing the grass – it's this kind of view that makes us think cows live simple lives with not much going on in their minds, but this isn't the truth. Cows are actually very social animals, capable of deep feelings for one another. They even have best friends!

Stressed out

If a cow is ever separated from its bestie, it can become stressed and its heart rate increases. If this separation goes on for too long it can affect the cow's milk production! Once it's reunited with its pal, a cow's heart rate lowers and its milk yield returns to normal. Happy cow, happy life!

1.5 BILLION

The number of cows in the world today.

Show me love

Did you know that cows who have been given names and are shown enough affection will return the love with an increased milk production?

KOALA

Each day these measured marsupials manage to get their heads down for between **20** and **22 hours**.

SLOTH

Every day these tardy tree-dwellers take way more than forty winks and sleep for **20 hours**.

SOME ANIMALS SPEND MOST OF THEIR LIVES ASLEEP

BROWN BAT

These mouse-eared microbats spend almost the whole day hanging upside-down asleep – sometimes for up to **20 hours**.

GIANT ARMADILLO

Each day these heavily armoured animals manage to rest their weary heads for around **18 hours**.

Humans tend to sleep for around **eight hours**, which is about a **third** of their lives spent sleeping. This may sound like quite a lot, but it's nothing when compared to some animals who spend most of their lives unconscious!

WOMBATS POOP CUBES

Wombats are the only animals that we know of who produce cube-shaped faeces. Cubic poop! They leave these very dry little poop cubes everywhere they go, not in an attempt to build little brick houses, but rather to mark their territory and communicate with other wombats.

Gut feeling

The reason for these cubic poops lies in the wombat's irregularly shaped intestines, which are a mind-blowing **nine metres** in length! That's huge, much bigger than a human's, and bonkers when you consider the small size of a wombat. As food passes through a wombat's long gut, these grooved intestines shape it into poop cubes.

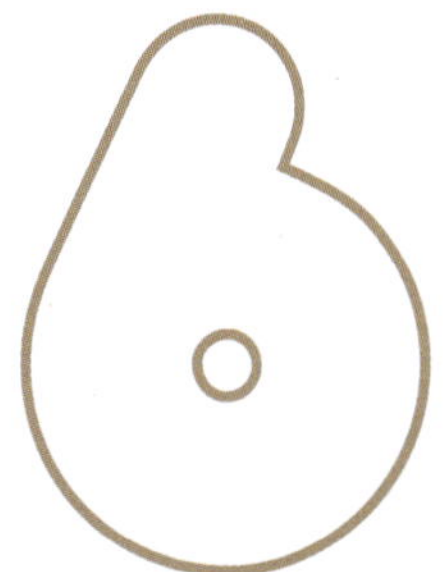

The number of days it takes a wombat to digest its food.

Up to speed

When they're not eating or pooping, wombats tend to waddle around, but if threatened they can really get a wriggle on. Wombats can sprint at speeds of up to **40 kilometres per hour** and do so for up to **90 seconds** at a time!

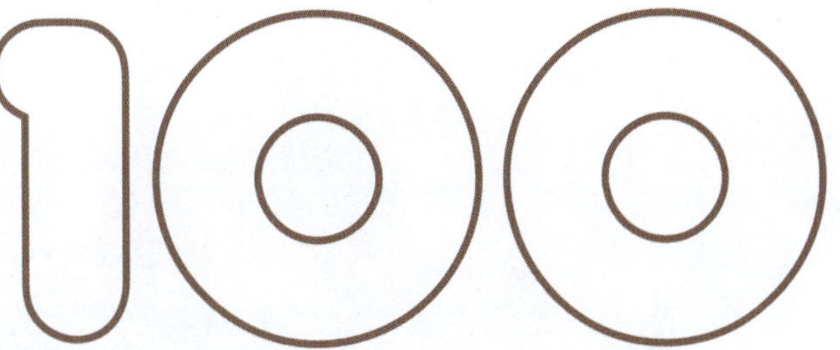

The number of poop cubes that a wombat can produce daily.

Giving it large

2.5 million years ago, the wombats in Australia would have looked a little different. They would have been the size of a rhinoceros! This mega wombat was called the **Diprotodon**, and weighed a staggering **2700 kilograms** and stretched **4 metres** from nose to tail. Just imagine how big those poop cubes would have been!

SEA TURTLES HAVE BEEN AROUND FOR A VERY, VERY LONG TIME

It's mind-bending to think that dinosaurs and sea turtles actually lived alongside each other. As sea turtles are still happily swimming in the world's oceans today, that means that these incredible creatures managed to outlive the dinosaurs. No way!

Chip off the old block

Fossils show turtles first started swimming **110 million years ago**. These swimming turtles descended from land turtles and freshwater turtles who existed approximately **230 million years ago**. This gives turtles an older fossil history than any other living four-legged animal.

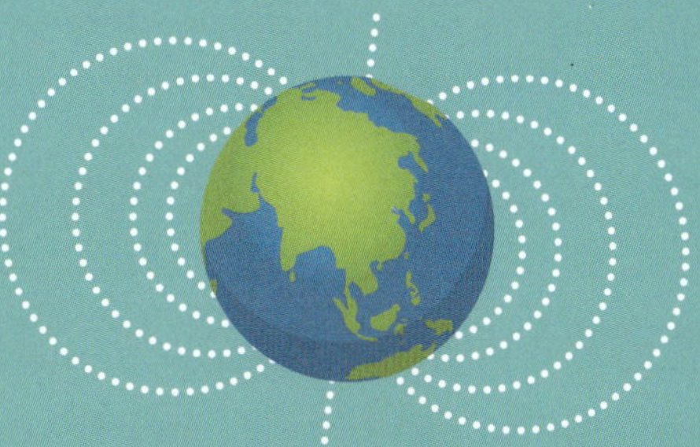

Magnetic attraction

Sea turtles have a compass inside their brains. They have the amazing ability to use the Earth's magnetic field to navigate vast distances across the oceans, sometimes up to **16,000 kilometres** every year.

Front-row seat

While undergoing relatively few evolutionary changes themselves, turtles have witnessed stunning changes elsewhere including the evolution of birds from feathered dinosaurs and the development of early mammals into elephants, whales, bats and even humans! Turtles have had a front-row seat at the evolutionary show!

100

The age that sea turtles can live to, and also roughly the number of eggs they lay each time they nest.

THS

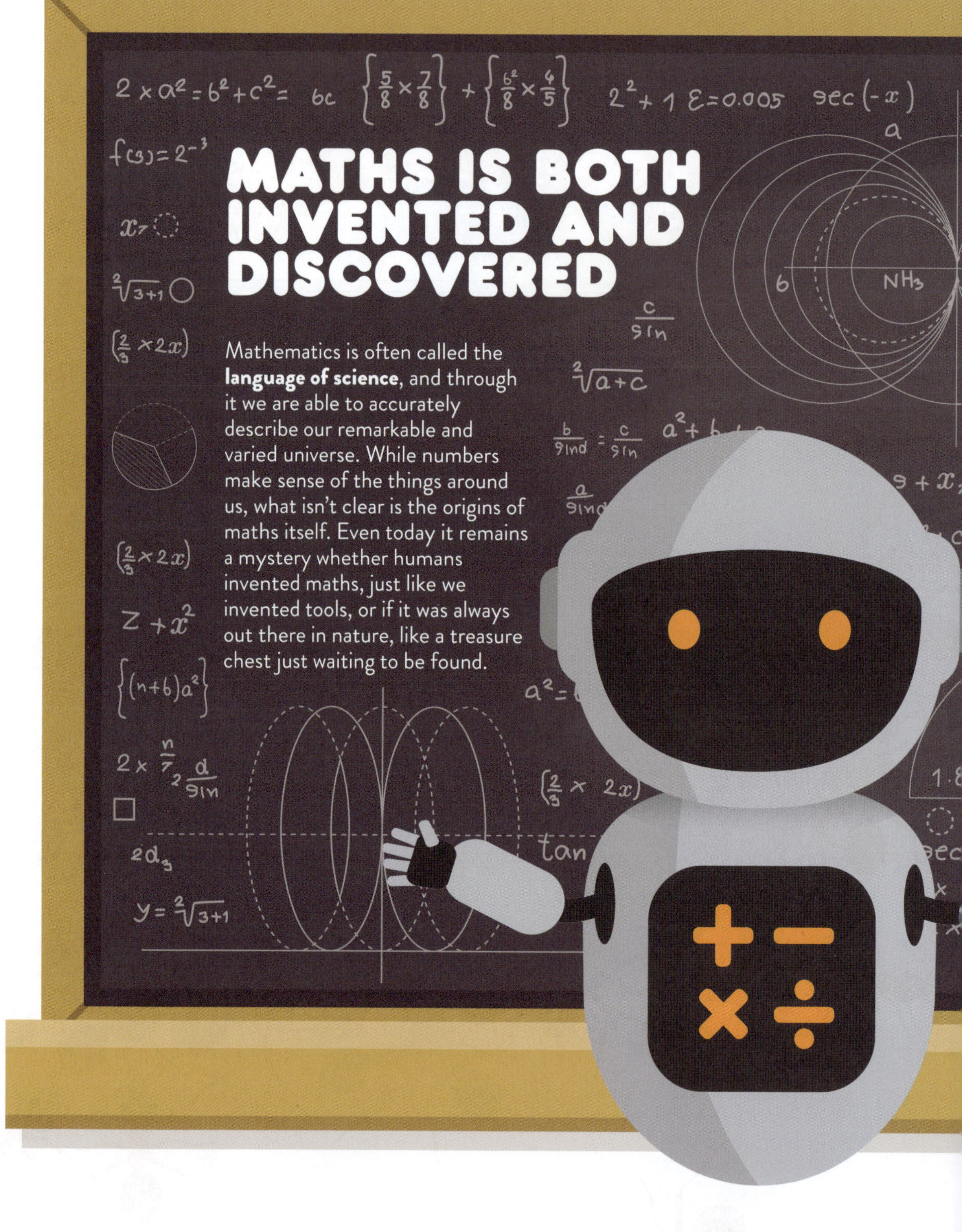

MATHS IS BOTH INVENTED AND DISCOVERED

Mathematics is often called the **language of science**, and through it we are able to accurately describe our remarkable and varied universe. While numbers make sense of the things around us, what isn't clear is the origins of maths itself. Even today it remains a mystery whether humans invented maths, just like we invented tools, or if it was always out there in nature, like a treasure chest just waiting to be found.

The foundations

Those who believe mathematics was discovered by humans also believe that maths is the foundation of everything, and the structure that supports our entire universe! These people believe maths is native to nature, and that if our universe was to disappear tomorrow it would still exist. By discovering maths, we have been able to begin to understand the physical world around us.

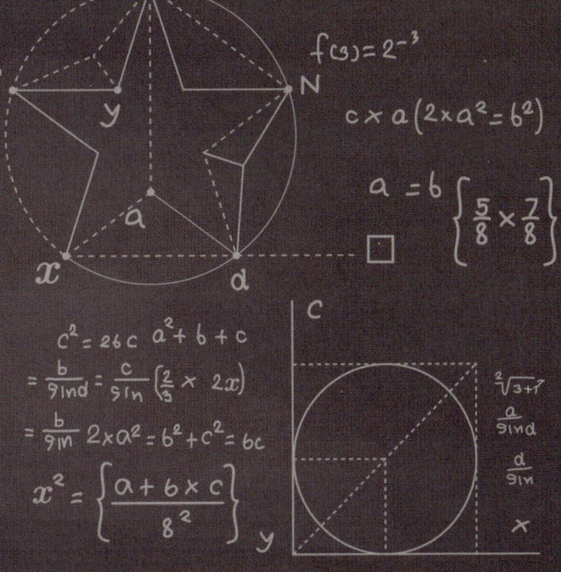

Making it all up

Those who believe humans invented maths argue that the only reason it is so well-suited to describing the physical world is because we designed it to do just that! These people argue that maths is straight out of our heads, and that we make it up as we go along, just to suit our own purposes. For them, if the universe was to vanish, there would be no more maths, just as there would be no more football, rugby, card games or anything else with rules humans have manufactured.

SOLVING SHAPE PUZZLES CAN IMPROVE YOUR MATHS SKILLS

If you like solving shape puzzles, then you might be interested to hear that doing so can improve your score in a maths test! Children who solved shape-rotation puzzles in the **40 minutes** prior to an arithmetic test generally achieved better results in that test.

Cut up

A **tangram** is a 200-year-old Chinese rearrangement puzzle that is made by cutting a square into seven **geometric shapes** called **tans**. The seven shapes are:

2 large right triangles
1 medium-sized right triangle
2 small right triangles
1 small square
1 parallelogram

When these shapes are arranged correctly, they fit together and form a large square, rectangle or triangle.

Get in shape

As well as forming shapes, tangrams can be arranged in many different formations to create some wonderful configurations, like the ones below:

Do you think that you could make just one cut to divide the shape to my left into two identical parts? It may sound impossible, but here's a clue: this shape is made of two identical shapes. Try to partition the big shape into two! The answer is on my screen.

ALWAYS ORDER THE LARGE PIZZA

If you're ever looking at a pizza menu with a grumbly tummy, your hungry stomach may tell you to order two mediums over a single large one, but mathematics tells us that one large pizza is actually bigger than two medium pizzas, which means more pizza on your plate (and usually for less money)!

A large pizza has a diameter of around **45 cm**.

The **radius** is half the diameter. On a large pizza the radius would be about **22.5 cm**.

To calculate the total area of a pizza, we use the following formula:
π **x radius**^{2}

π **x 22.5**^{2}

All this information tells us that the total area of large pizza is **1590 cm**^{2}.

Sweet as pi

π is the symbol for the number called Pi and represents the ratio of a circle's **circumference** (length around a circle) to its **diameter** (distance from one side of a circle to the opposite side). Pi goes on forever, but it's approximately equal to **3.14159265358979323846** ... Because this number is infinite, we usually abbreviate it to **3.14**.

30 cm

A medium pizza has a diameter of **30 cm**, and a radius of **15 cm**.

Using our formula from the large pizza, we know that we use π x $\mathbf{15^2}$ to calculate the total area of the pizza.

The total area of a medium pizza is **707 cm²**.

The total area of two medium pizzas is **1414 cm²**, which is **176 cm** *less* than the large pizza.

So, if you're hungry, always order the large pizza!

PATTERNS OF NUMBERS ARE HIDDEN IN NATURE

Did you know that the mathematician **Fibonacci** discovered a sequence of numbers that exists in nature? The order is as follows: **0**, **1**, **1**, **2**, **3**, **5**, **8**, **13**, **21**, **34**, **55**, **89**, **144**, and continues on to infinity. Each new number in the sequence is the total of the previous two numbers, and they are known as the **Fibonacci numbers** or the **Fibonacci sequence.** The ratio between the numbers (**1.618034**) is frequently called the **golden ratio** or **golden number**.

Did you know ratios compare values? They tell us how much of one thing there is compared to another.

Nature's call

Nature is full of the Fibonacci sequence. The spiral patterns that you see in sunflowers and pinecones all have the sequence and golden ratio, as do pineapples and cauliflowers. The sequence appears in the way plants arrange their leaves, a pattern which gives them maximum exposure to light, just as flowers use Fibonacci for maximum seed arrangement.

Body count

It's not just plants that showcase these patterns; most of our human body parts follow the numbers **1**, **2**, **3** and **5**. We have one nose, two eyes, three sections to each limb and five fingers on each hand.

Spiral round

The golden ratio is expressed in spiralling shells. In this illustration, areas of the shell's growth are mapped out in squares. If the two smallest squares have a width and height of one square, then the box to their left has measurements of two. The other boxes measure 3, 5, 8 and 13.

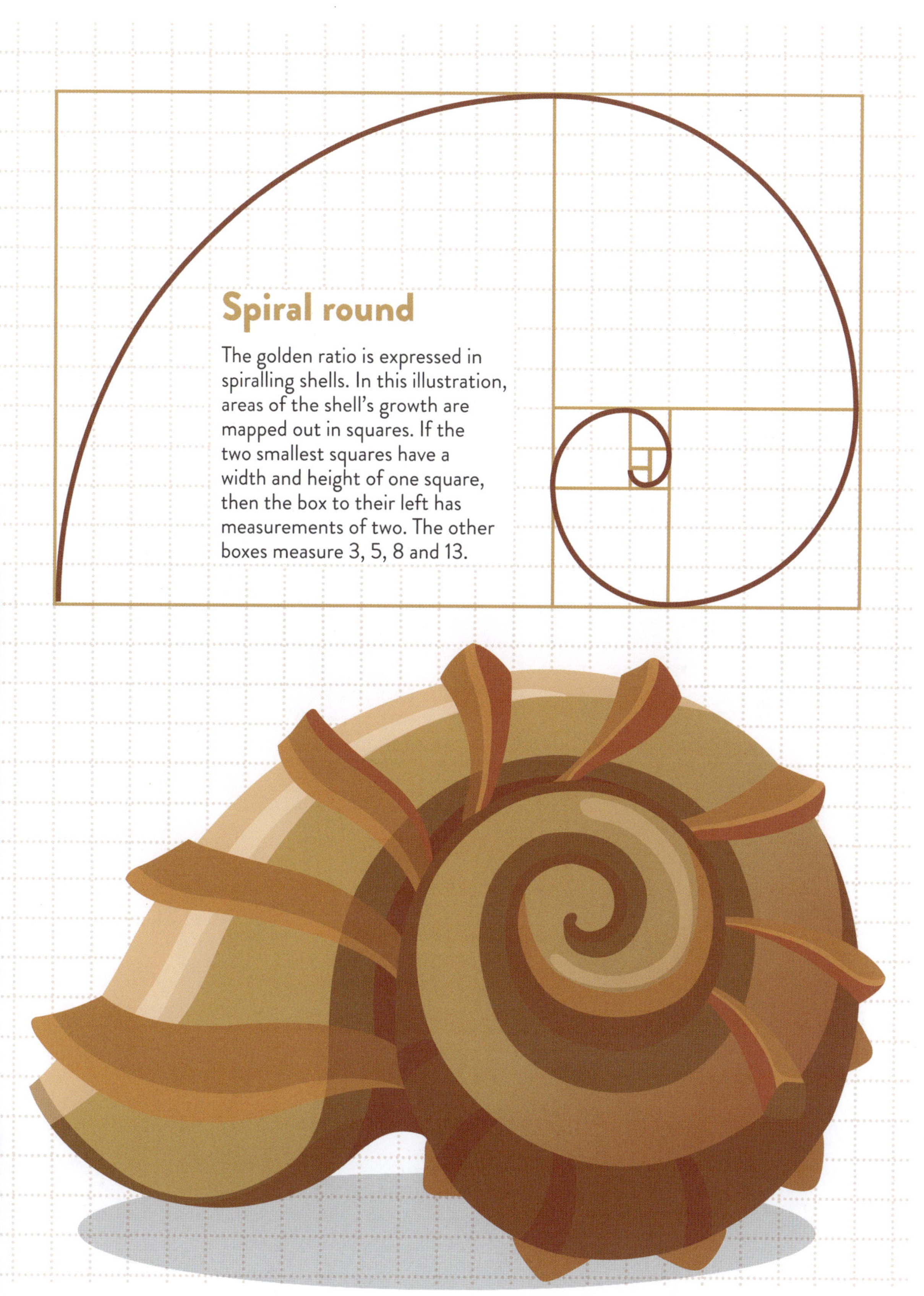

CAN YOU CONNECT ALL THESE DOTS WITH JUST FOUR LINES?

See if you can connect all **nine dots** with no more than **four straight lines**. Each dot is not to be connected more than once, and you have to do it all without lifting your hand from the paper. KLAUS has the answer below!

MATHS CHALLENGE

FRACTALS GO ON FOREVER

Trying to picture something **infinite** (that means something that has no end and goes on forever and ever) is amazingly difficult – it can make your brain hurt just thinking about it! A great way to help contemplate the size of infinity is through **fractals**. A fractal is a never-ending pattern that repeats itself at different scales, which is known as **self-similarity**. Even though fractals can look fantastically complicated, they're really just made by repeating a simple process.

Zoom, zoom, zoom

Mathematical fractals are created by calculating a simple equation thousands of times, and then feeding those answers in a loop back to the beginning. These fractals are infinitely complicated and allow us to zoom into the fractal forever.

Eternal triangle

Another mathematical fractal is the **Sierpiński triangle**, named after the mathematician Wacław Sierpiński. This is a **self-similar fractal** and is made from a triangle with equal sides, inside of which smaller equal-sided triangles are repeatedly removed in a repeating pattern.

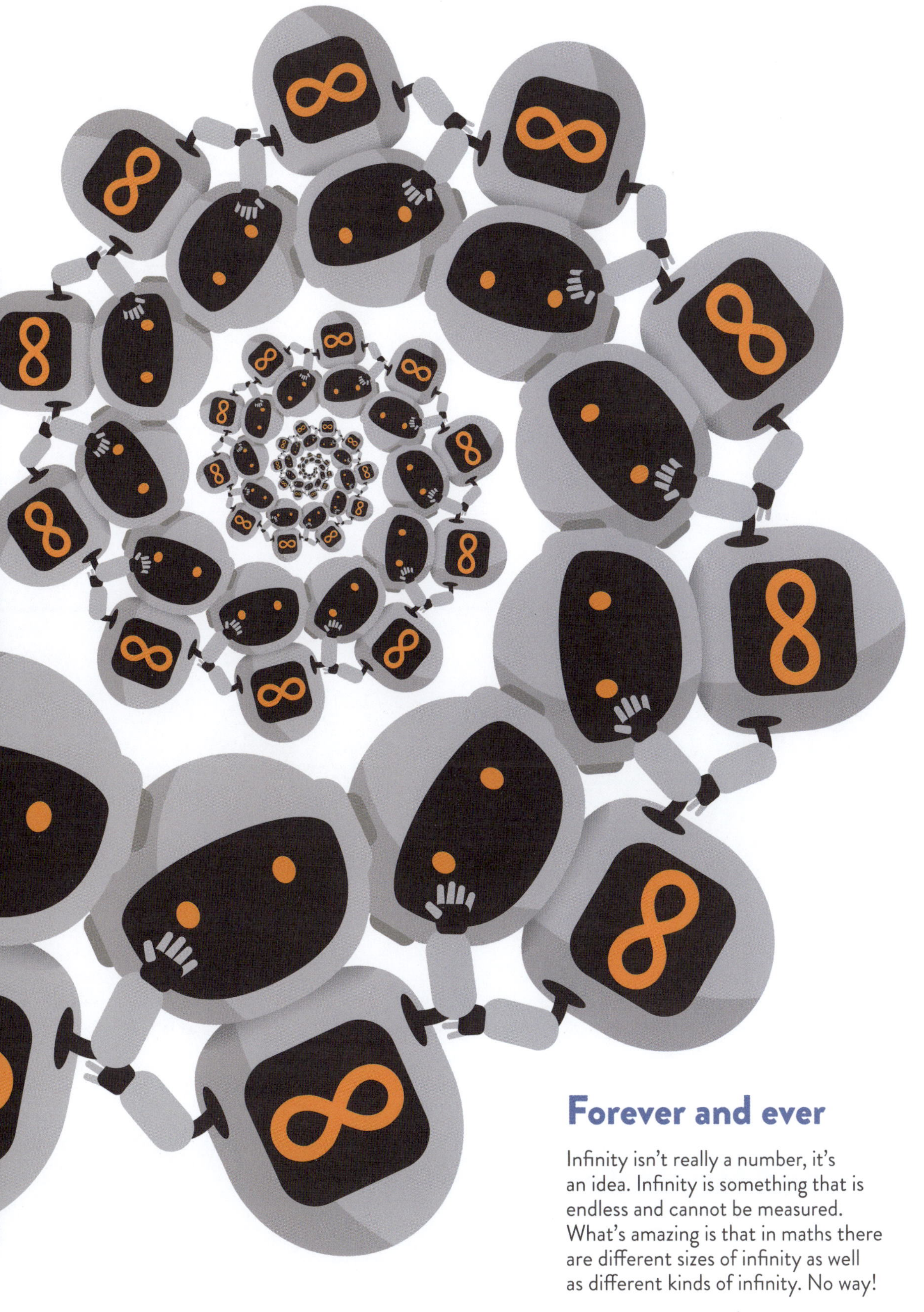

Forever and ever

Infinity isn't really a number, it's an idea. Infinity is something that is endless and cannot be measured. What's amazing is that in maths there are different sizes of infinity as well as different kinds of infinity. No way!

THERE IS AN EQUATION FOR FINDING ALIENS

Somewhat certain

$$N = R \times f_p \times n_e$$

Number of technologically advanced civilisations in the Milky Way galaxy.

Rate of formation of stars in the galaxy.

Fraction of those stars with planetary systems.

Number of planets per solar system with environment suitable for life.

In 1961, an amazing mathematical formula was proposed, and, if calculated, it could estimate the number of contactable alien civilisations in our Milky Way galaxy! This formula was devised by astronomer **Frank Drake** and is known as the **Drake Equation**.

Considering the massive size of the Milky Way galaxy and the hundreds of billions of solar systems within it, there is every chance that we are not alone in the universe. If aliens are in fact out there, then Frank Drake developed an incredibly brilliant way to start calculating how many of them there could be. Scientists say the Drake Equation is a difficult formula to work with, as it contains too many unknown elements. However, they do agree the real importance of the equation is not in solving it, but in thinking about it in the first place.

Extremely uncertain

Fraction of suitable planets on which life actually appears.

Fraction of life-bearing planets on which intelligent life emerges.

Fractions of civilisations that develop a technology that releases detectable signs of their existence into space.

Length of time such civilisations release detectable signs of their existence into space.

WHAT'S THE NEXT NUMBER IN THIS SEQUENCE?

MATHS CHALLENGE

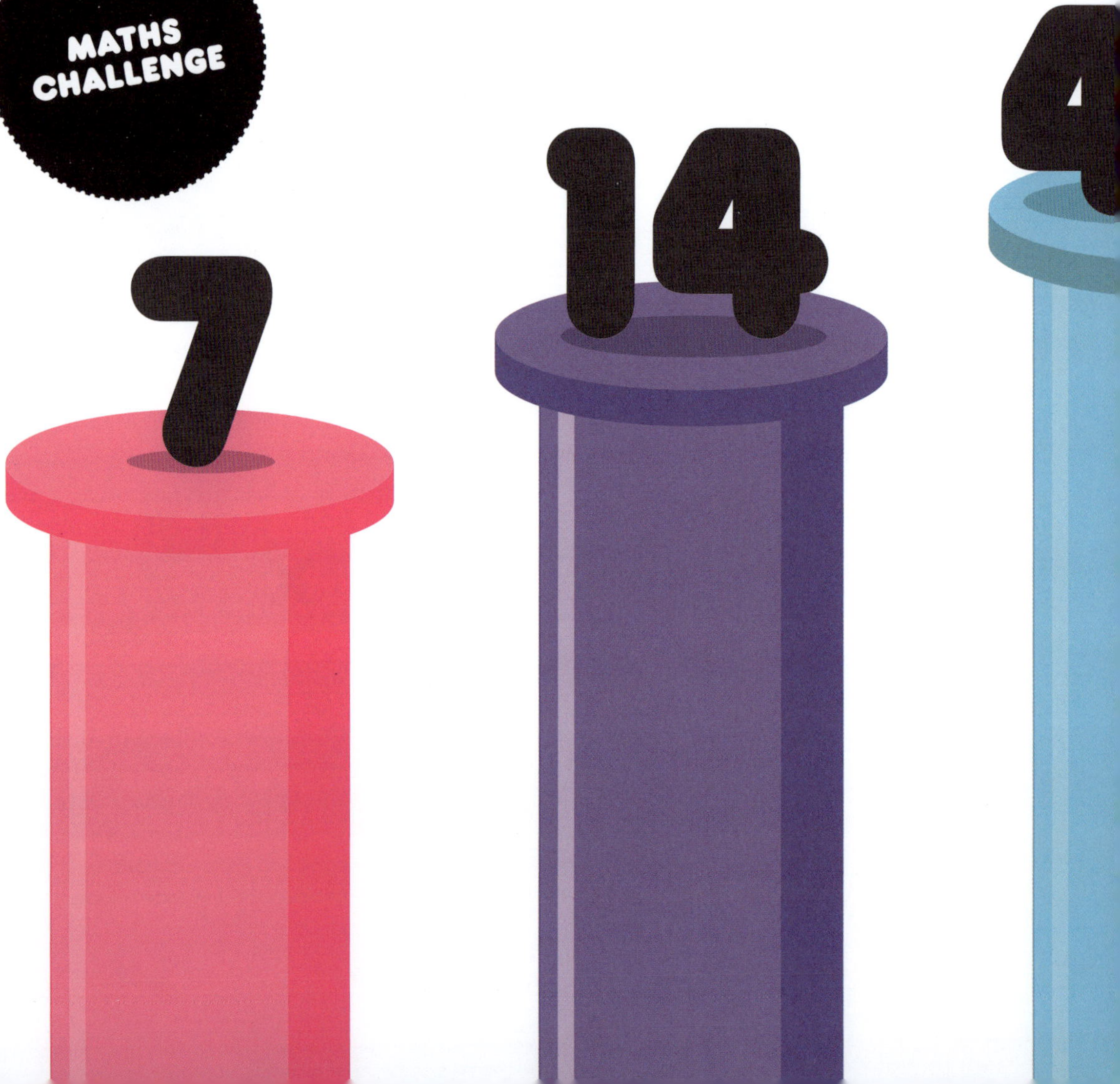

7

14

4

A good hint for solving number sequence puzzles is to see if any of the numbers can be divided by another. If they can, you might be able to see a pattern emerge. Good luck!

Answer: **840.** Each new number in the sequence is found by multiplying the number that corresponds to its pillar by the number of pillars that proceed it.

WHEN YOU SHUFFLE THAT EXACT ORDER BEFORE IN THE HISTO

There are **52 playing cards** in a deck. That number in itself isn't anything to get too excited about, but if you were to give that deck a shuffle and lay those 52 cards down in a line that number would start to get *a lot* more exciting! Each time you reshuffle those cards and lay them out again, you'd be creating a combination that has never been seen before!

Spoiled for choice

If you look at the maths behind it, a deck of 52 cards can be ordered like this:

52 x **51** x **50** x **49** x ... x **3** x **2** x **1**. To express this in words, there are **52** ways to choose the first card, **51** ways to choose the second, **50** ways to choose the third, and so on.

The number of order possibilities that result is:

80,658,175,170,943,878,571, 660,636,856,403,766,975,28 9,505,440 883,277,824,000, 000,000,000

Or, if ridiculously large numbers make your head fall off, $\mathbf{8 \times 10^{67}}$.

DECK OF CARDS,
S NEVER BEEN SEEN
Y OF THE UNIVERSE

Seeing stars

The number of possible orders is big. It's bigger than astronomical. It's so big that it even goes beyond cosmic! In fact, it's bigger than the total number of all the stars in the universe!

Once in a lifetime

With this beyond-cosmic number of possibilities in mind, it's a safe bet that any order of cards drawn through random shuffling is likely to never have appeared before – and to never appear again in your lifetime!

The universal truth

This number of possibilities is so massive that if someone had been shuffling a deck of cards once every second since the beginning of the universe – over **14 billion years ago** – they wouldn't have even shuffled the deck **10^{18}** times.

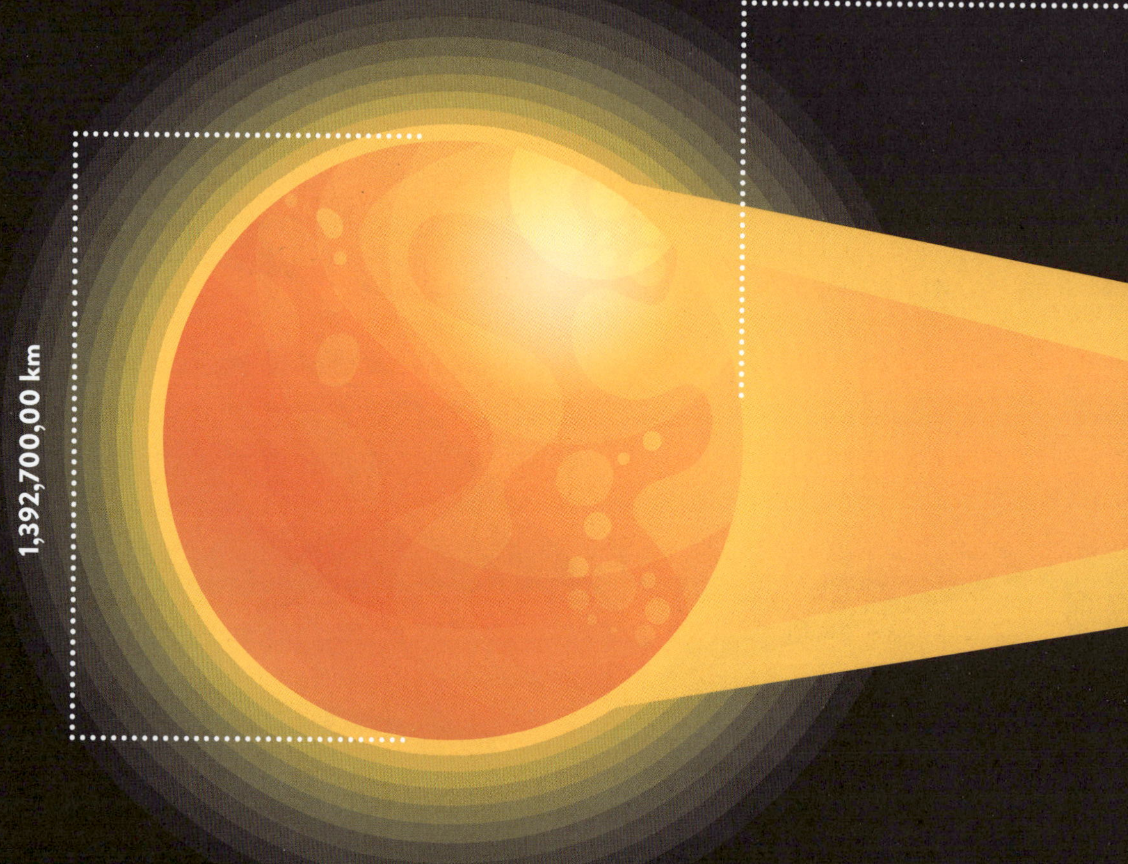

TOTAL SOLAR ECLIPSES ARE THANKS TO LUCKY MATHS

A solar eclipse happens when the moon slowly passes between the Sun and Earth. An eclipse is a strange moment that causes the temperature to drop and the sky to go dark in the middle of the day. It's an epic sight, and there is an equally extraordinary numerical coincidence that allows it to happen, and it's all down to the number **400**.

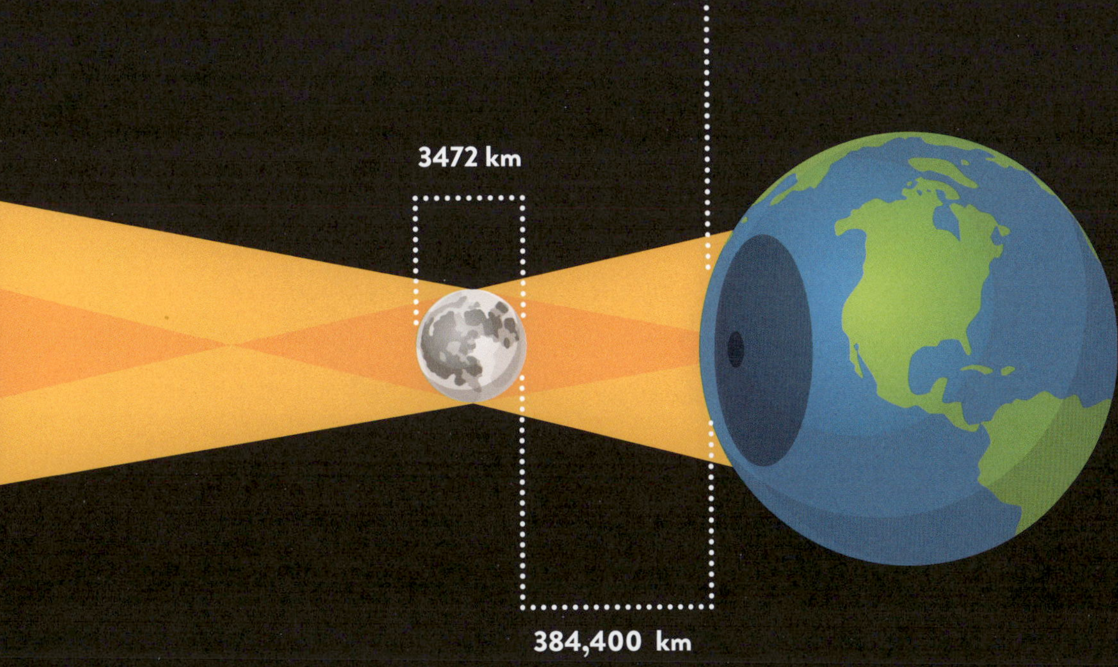

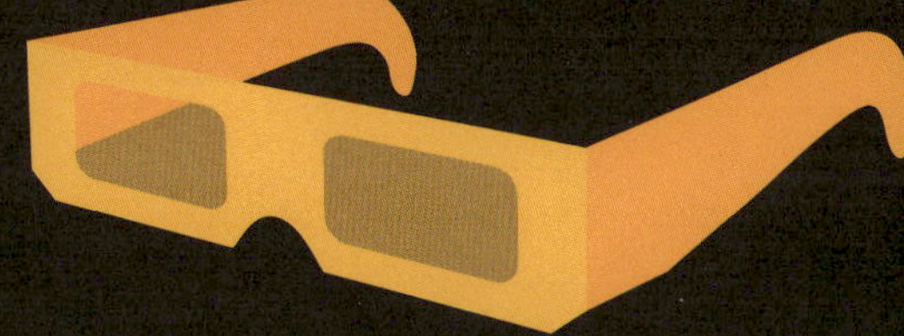

The diameter of the Sun is about **400 times larger** than the diameter of the Moon. But, by an amazing cosmic coincidence, the Sun is about **400 times further away** from Earth than the Moon. As things appear smaller the further away they are, this means that down here on Earth, the Sun and Moon appear to be roughly the same size. Amazing!

Glassy eyed

If you are ever lucky enough to see all the stages of a solar eclipse, make sure you wear special eclipse glasses – these are dark filters in a cardboard frame that protect your retinas from the potential UV damage caused by staring at the Sun, even during an eclipse – for protection!

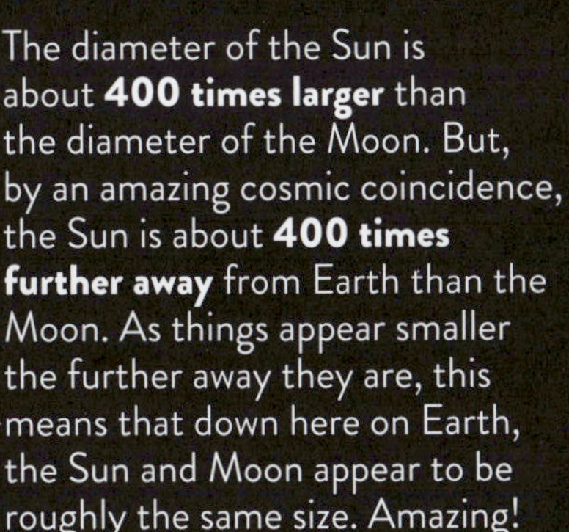

MATHS CHALLENGE

HOW MANY TRIANGLES CAN YOU SEE HERE?

The coloured hexagonal shape above contains a number of triangles. Look very closely. Can you see them all? KLAUS has the answers on the opposite page, but no sneaky peeks! To help count the triangles grab a penciland paper and draw them as you see them!

Total number of triangles: **35**

TRILLION

A MILLION, A BILLION AND A TRILLION AREN'T REMOTELY SIMILAR IN SIZE

People tend to group big numbers together; maybe it's because they look similar, or maybe it's because they rhyme. But, thinking that big numbers come in groups could not be further from the truth, especially in the case of a **million, billion** and **trillion**. In case you're unsure, a **billion** is a **thousand millions** (**1,000,000,000**) and a **trillion** is a **thousand billions** (**1,000,000,000,000**).

BILLION MILLION

Get rich quick

Look at it this way: if you were able to earn a dollar every second you were alive, you'd be an infant **millionaire** in little under two weeks, complete with gold-lined nappies. After hitting your precocious millionaire-peak, you'd be waiting until you were **31 years old** to make **billionaire** status. But, sadly, those dreams of becoming a **trillionaire** would never come true, as it would take a shocking **32,000 years** to achieve that level of wealth.

Sky high

Here's another way of looking at it. If you took your infant wealth and changed your theoretical millions into crisp one-dollar bills, your million-dollar stack would be the height of a chair. It's not surprising that your billion-dollar pile would be much more impressive, soaring a kilometre into the sky – even higher than the Burj Khalifa, the world's current largest building!

Leave home

Even more impressive would be your unachievable trillion-dollar pile. As this builds up, it would leave its Earthly confines, stretching **1000 kilometres** up – way past the Kármán line (the altitude where space begins). It would pass the International Space Station (ISS) and keep going until it was two-and-a-half-times that distance from Earth!

CALCULATING PERCENTAGES

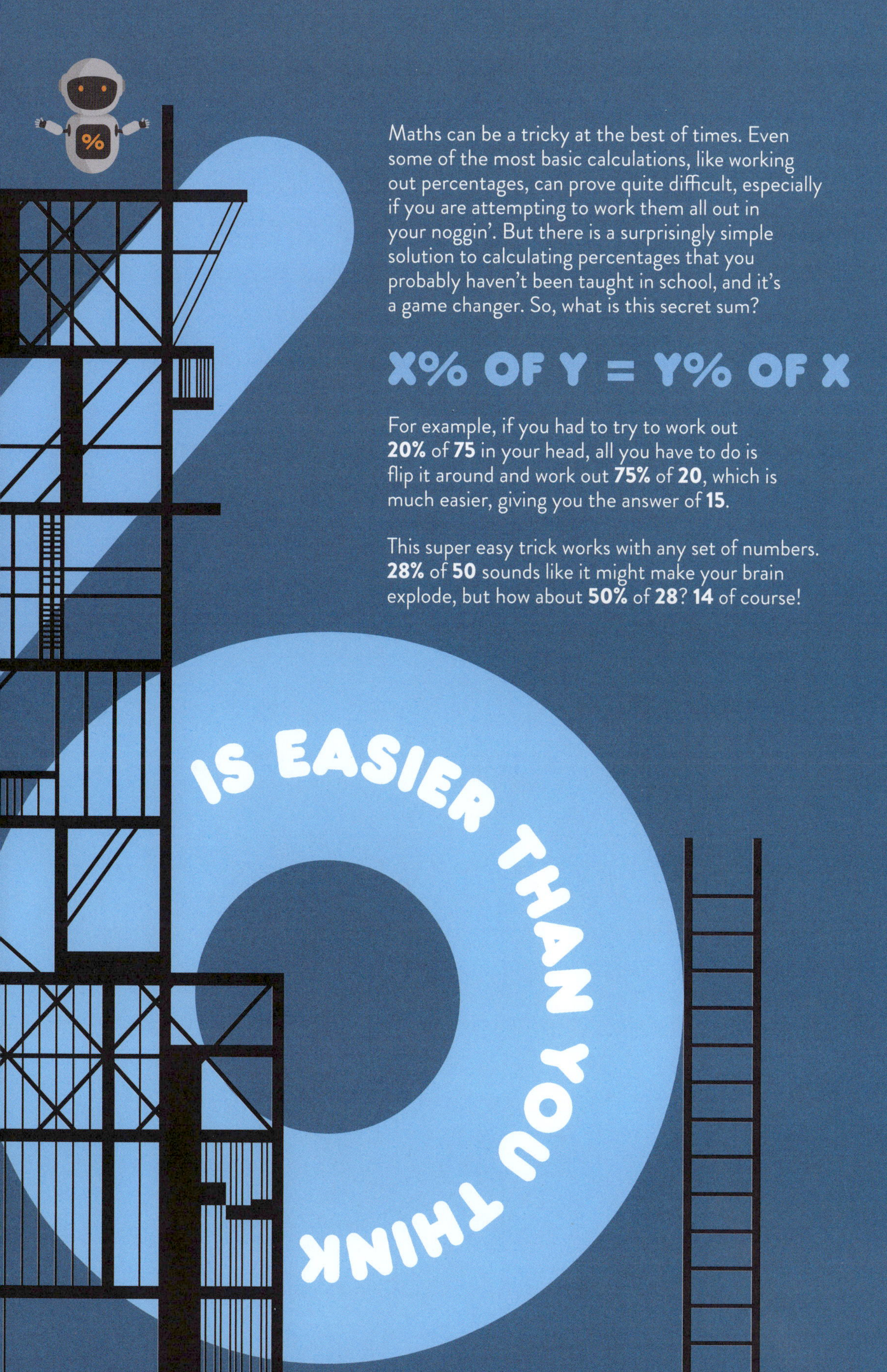

Maths can be a tricky at the best of times. Even some of the most basic calculations, like working out percentages, can prove quite difficult, especially if you are attempting to work them all out in your noggin'. But there is a surprisingly simple solution to calculating percentages that you probably haven't been taught in school, and it's a game changer. So, what is this secret sum?

X% OF Y = Y% OF X

For example, if you had to try to work out **20%** of **75** in your head, all you have to do is flip it around and work out **75%** of **20**, which is much easier, giving you the answer of **15**.

This super easy trick works with any set of numbers. **28%** of **50** sounds like it might make your brain explode, but how about **50%** of **28**? **14** of course!

WHAT'S THE MISSING NUMBER?

The coloured circle here has seven numbers, but can you figure out what the eighth number is?

Answer: **20.** The numbers opposite one another must total **24.**

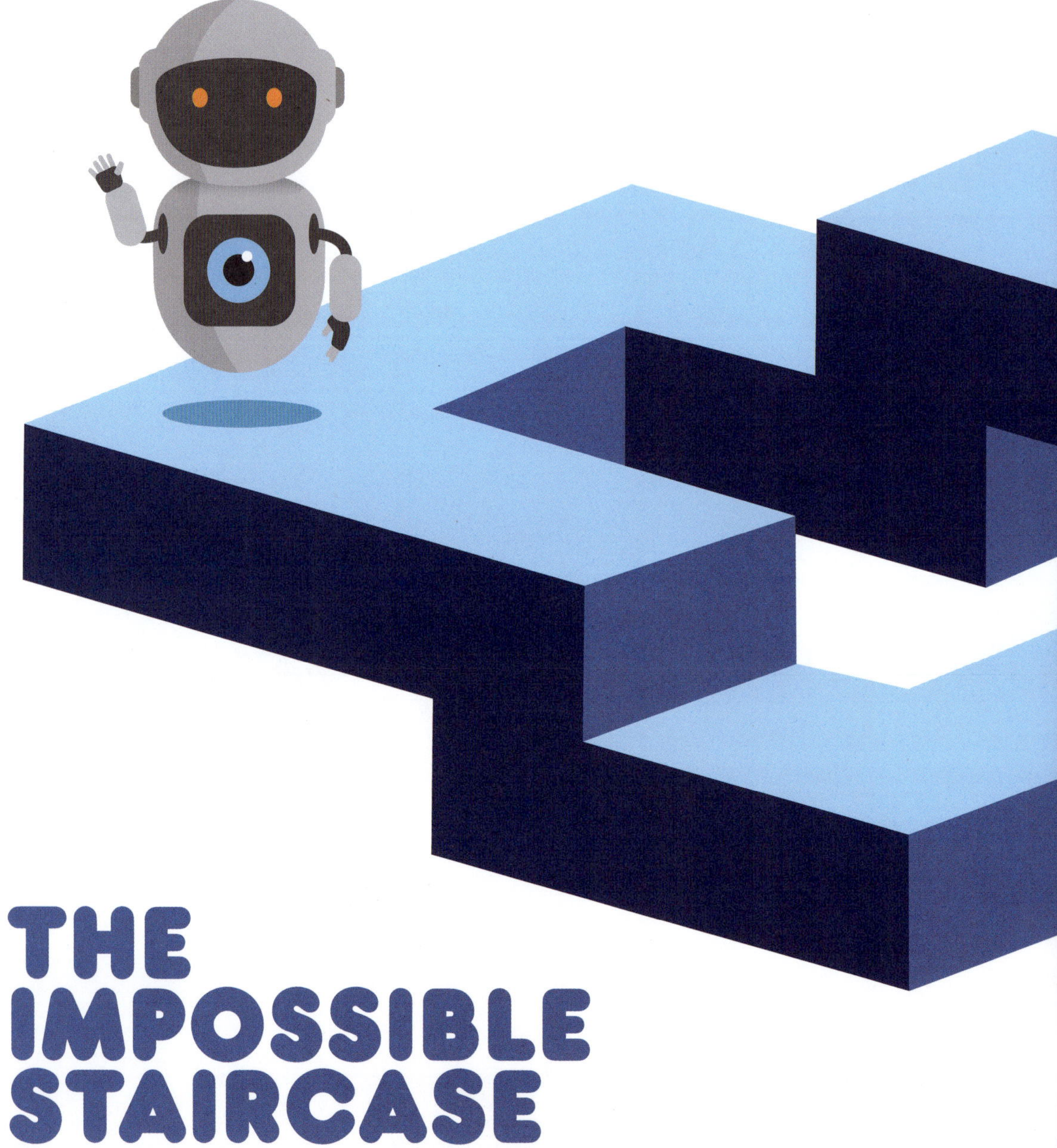

THE IMPOSSIBLE STAIRCASE

At first glance, the steps above look like any other staircase, but when you follow the stairs you'll realise the whole structure is impossible! Any person who dared to use these stairs would be climbing up or going down them forever! This illustration is an example of an **impossible object**, and was designed by Swedish graphic artist, Oscar Reutersvärd.

Upstairs downstairs

Another impossible object is **the Penrose staircase** and was created by mathematician Lionel Penrose and his son Roger after they were inspired by the Dutch graphic artist M.C. Escher.

Under the illusion

In order to further bend our minds, the Penroses also created the **impossible triangle**. This is another mind-bending mathematical object that creates an optical illusion which can be represented in a perspective drawing, but can never exist as a solid object in the real world.

CICADAS USE PRIME NUMBERS

A prime number is a whole number greater than **1** that can't be made by multiplying other whole numbers. For example, 5 is a prime number, as are **2**, **7**, **11**, **13**, **53** and **71**. This mathematical quality may not sound particularly unique, but prime numbers are pretty special. Especially to cicadas!

Going underground

If you've ever lain in bed during a summer's night, unable to sleep thanks to the cacophonous din of cicadas, then you're probably not a fan of these flying insects. Their life cycle is a strange one, as they spend most of their days underground, and when they do finally emerge there's no time for pleasantries as they quickly find a mate, reproduce and die.

7, 13, 17

Annual cicadas make an appearance every year, but periodic cicadas stay underground for much longer, emerging at intervals of **7**, **13** or even **17** years, all of which are prime numbers!

Syncing up

Another benefit of the strategically irregular gaps in the appearance of cicadas is that they prevent predators syncing up with their reproductive cycles. A predator with a 3-year life cycle would only meet up with the 17-year periodic cicadas once every **51** years.

Taking advantage

Could it be a coincidence that cicadas use prime numbers? For a long time we thought so, but now it seems that these insect mathematicians have been using prime numbers to their advantage all along, and without the help of a calculator!

Food fight

For instance, cicadas with a **13-year life cycle** and ones with a **17-year life cycle** will hardly ever meet. When both species of cicada do come out together – once every **221 years** – the numbers will be massive, so it's handy they rarely have to compete for the same food.

SOME NUMBERS ARE BIGGER THAN THE UNIVERSE

In order to describe the enormity of the universe we have to use some very large numbers. It is almost **14 billion years** old and spans **93 billion light years** across. But there are some numbers which are actually bigger than the universe itself. Much bigger. In fact, they are so big that there isn't enough space in the universe to write them down!

MATHS CHALLENGE

See if you can write down a googol. Take your time and be careful counting those zeros.

Googol

As well as sounding like a very popular search engine, (which is actually misnamed after a googol) a **googol** is the number **one** followed by **100 zeros**, or $\mathbf{10^{100}}$. If you compare a googol with the number of atoms in the observable universe it is obviously much larger.

Up and atom

Atoms are the building blocks for every single thing in the universe – the stars, planets, comets and asteroids. Scientists have calculated that the total number of atoms there are in the observable universe is anything up to $\mathbf{10^{82}}$. That is a **one** followed by **82 zeros**!

Googolplex

A googol is big, but a **googleplex** is bigger. It is written as $\mathbf{10^{googol}}$. It is so huge that it is too big for the universe to accommodate! There literally isn't enough space or time in the universe to write down a googolplex. Even if you were to write two zeros every second, it would still take much, much longer than the age of the universe to finish writing out a googolplex!

Did you enjoy the book? Is your brain bouncing with fantastic new facts and figures? Don't worry if you couldn't understand everything. That's what's great about learning – sometimes it takes time, but it's always worth it!

There's always something new to learn about the universe we live in, so keep your eyes and ears open! When you do discover something new and wonderful, make sure you share it with someone else!

Goodbye, for now.

About the author

Dan Marshall is a designer, illustrator and writer who has been drawing since he was a young child. It never fails to surprise him that as a grown-up he's now paid to do just that. Dan has created graphics for Sydney Opera House, The Australian Museum and Facebook.

Dan's first book, *Mind Blown*, was born from his passion for graphic design, communicating information visually and his deep curiosity for the incredibly strange place that is our universe. Dan's second book, *Look Book*, was published in 2021, and is for readers aged zero to three. *No Way!* is his third book.